Low-Income Housing: A Critique of Federal Aid

Robert Taggart III

The Johns Hopkins Press, Baltimore and London

Copyright © 1970 by The Johns Hopkins Press
All rights reserved
Manufactured in the United States of America

The Johns Hopkins Press, Baltimore, Maryland 21218
The Johns Hopkins Press Ltd., London

Library of Congress Catalog Card Number   70–134301

International Standard Book Number 0-8018-1248-8 (clothbound edition)
International Standard Book Number 0-8018-1249-6 (paperback edition)

Originally published, 1970
Paperback edition, 1970

This study was prepared under a grant from The Ford Foundation.

Contents

List of Tables

List of Charts

Preface

Millions of Americans live in substandard, overcrowded or delapidated homes, and their squalid environment contributes to many
of our most serious social problems. Conditions are improving,
as the number of ill-housed is gradually declining, but further
and faster improvements are needed.

To hasten progress toward the national goal of "a decent home
and suitable living environment for every American family," Congress authorized the construction and subsidization of six million
units for low- and moderate-income families over the decade
beginning in 1968. In the last two years, production has increased
markedly, but it has still lagged far behind targetted rates. Over the
rest of the decade, the federal effort to build and subsidize low-cost
housing will have to and can be expected to expand.

This effort involves the use of a number of separate housing
subsidy programs which provide alternative and complementary
approaches to the complex needs of the ill-housed. These programs
must be improved, their application rationalized, and increased
emphasis given to those with the greatest impact, if the most effective use is to be made of expanding housing funds.

This study analyzes the existing federal subsidy programs. It reviews their intended purposes and accomplishments to date, and it suggests ways they should be used and improved in the future.

Many people contributed to this study. Without exception, personnel in the Department of Agriculture and especially the Department of Housing and Urban Development have been extremely co-operative. Henry Schechter of HUD and Harold Havens of the Bureau of the Budget provided careful readings and many helpful suggestions. Linda Walters contributed in many intangible as well as tangible ways. But, most of all, Sar A. Levitan provided guidance from beginning to end. I am deeply indebted to him for his understanding and patient tutelage.

The study was prepared under a grant from The Ford Foundation to The George Washington University's Center for Manpower Policy Studies. In accordance with the Foundation's practice, complete responsibility for the preparation of the volume was left to the author.

ROBERT TAGGART III

Low-Income Housing

1

Overview

Housing problems have grown more serious and widespread, so that almost everyone is affected. Costs have spiralled while quality has seemingly declined. Credit is scarce and expensive, affecting both builders and buyers. Vacancy rates have fallen to rock-bottom levels, restricting residential mobility. And, worst of all, the present slump in housing construction means that housing shortages are likely to continue for several years.

These developments are perplexing and troublesome to the majority of Americans, but they are hardly overwhelming. Though we may feel that housing is too costly, that interest rates are too high, and that new homes and apartments are too difficult to find, most of us can make temporary adjustments with a fair degree of certainty that improvements will be forthcoming. Some continue to live in their present dwellings, postponing home purchases or moves to newer units. Others settle for less than the home of their dreams. And many increase the proportion of income spent on housing. Everyone would like cheaper, better quality, and more readily available housing than exists under present conditions, but most of us do not suffer excessively.

For a large minority, however, current developments have intensified problems which were already severe. This minority includes the millions of American families who live in substandard, overcrowded or delapidated housing. According to the 1960 Census, 18 percent of all occupied homes were substandard, based on a definition which would count almost any watertight building with indoor plumbing as standard. An additional 8 percent were described as "deteriorating" and were for the most part barely livable; 12 percent had more than one person per room and were so overcrowded that their occupants were undeniably ill-housed. These conditions are intolerable, and their elimination is the very least which should be done.

Most of the families living in these physically inadequate or overcrowded units are poor and almost all have a low income, even if they are above the poverty threshold. But there are also many low-income families occupying "standard" dwellings, though they must spend an excessive portion of their income. In 1967 about one in eight American households would have had to use more than one-fifth of their income for housing despite the fact that the average household spends only 15 percent. The millions who occupy minimally adequate shelter by paying an exorbitant share of their income also need help.

Whatever their exact number, these ill-housed and low-income households add up to a sizable segment of the population. For them, current housing conditions have intensified long-standing problems, making it even more difficult to find minimally adequate shelter. High costs, housing shortages, and inflated interest rates have been felt most severely by the families with the least income—those without the options which money provides.

The housing problems of the majority of Americans need more attention. Efforts must be made to expand mortgage funds, to lower interest rates, and to stimulate production so that the backlog of housing demand can be gradually met. Low-income families will benefit as housing markets loosen, vacancies increase, and the prices of older units fall; without such improvements their problems are made even more difficult to solve.

But even if general housing conditions improve, many families will

2

still be ill-housed. It takes a long time for improvements to trickle down from the rich to the poor; and if a construction boom took place now for middle- and upper-income housing, it would be years before low-cost markets would feel the effects with price reductions. Even then, many families would have too little income to afford adequate shelter. Theirs is the really serious and intransigent "housing problem."

Despite its intransigence, this low-income housing problem would probably disappear over several decades without any increased efforts. Poverty itself is being reduced and hopefully will be eliminated sometime in the future, so that all families can afford at least minimally standard dwellings. Income gains in the past have been associated with substantial reductions in the number and proportion of substandard units. They declined by almost one-third in the fifties—17.0 million units in 1950 to 11.4 million units in 1959—and progress continued in the sixties, with an estimated decline to 6.2 million substandard units at the end of 1968. A projection of the 1968 rates of deterioration and replacement estimated that only 3.8 million substandard units will remain at the end of the current decade.[1]

Nevertheless, the misery and social ills caused by poor housing are hardly mitigated by the long-run prospects of improvement. Early childhood in a squalid tenement can be permanently detrimental, and the damage may be done before better housing is provided at the present rates of progress. Even if all substandard housing is eliminated within twenty years, and even if we are willing to accept all the ill effects in the interim, our standards must surely change. If all housing units were suddenly made watertight with indoor plumbing, squalor, filth, decay, and especially the overcrowding which has increased in recent years, would remain, though the census-takers would find few substandard units. Anthony Downs put it this way in his careful analysis of housing goals and needs:

[1] National Commission on Urban Problems, *Building the American City* (Washington, D.C.: Government Printing Office, December 1968), p. 70.

According to the official national goal, every American household which does not enjoy "a decent home and a suitable environment" is part of the housing problem. Unfortunately, this statement utterly fails to convey the appalling living conditions which give the housing problem such overriding urgency to millions of poor Americans. In fact, most Americans have no conception of the filth, degradation, squalor, overcrowding and personal danger and insecurity which millions of inadequate housing units are causing in both our cities and rural areas. . . . Until you have actually stumbled through the ill-lit and decaying rooms of a slum dwelling, smelled the stench of sewage and garbage and dead rats behind the walls, seen the roaches and crumbling plaster and incredibly filthy bathrooms, and recoiled from exposed wiring and rotting floorboards and staircases, you have no real idea of what bad housing is like. These miserable conditions are not true of all inadequate housing units, but enough Americans are trapped in the hopeless desolation of such surroundings to constitute both a scandal and a serious economic and social drag in our affluent society.[2]

If the plight of the ill-housed is to be eased in the near future, we cannot sit back and wait for the effects of improved housing conditions to filter down to the poor or for income improvements which will permit them to compete for existing adequate units. The simple fact is that many millions of families now have, and will continue for some time to have, an income too low to afford minimally standard shelter. Without direct and increased assistance in meeting their housing needs they will continue to be ill-housed.

The responsibility for assisting those families lies almost entirely with the federal government. A few states and a few large metropolitan areas have played an active role, providing a variety of subsidies to low-income families and incentives to builders of low-cost housing. In New York City, for example, almost two-thirds of the subsidized housing units are financially assisted by the state or the city.[3] However, most state and local governments have in-

[2] Anthony Downs, "Moving Towards Realistic Housing Goals," *Agenda For The Nation* (Washington, D.C.: The Brookings Institution, 1968), pp. 141–42.

[3] First National City Bank of New York, "Government's Role in Housing," February 18, 1970. Mimeographed.

vested little of their resources in low-income housing, and even the most active have had to cut back their efforts in the face of rising prices and increasing fiscal burdens. For the most part, if low-income families are to be helped, increased assistance will be needed from the federal government.

To accelerate the solution of low-income housing problems, higher priority must be given at the national level. But when so many issues are demanding a larger share of national resources, each demand must be carefully weighed. Consideration must be given to the question of whether housing deserves more attention at the expense of other goods and services for low-income families, such as education, improved health care or income maintenance. Several factors, however, weigh in favor of an expanded housing effort, even if this means that other goals cannot be expanded. First, federal housing programs have consistently fallen short of their recognized needs and solemnly declared goals, so that housing problems which could have been solved continue to plague us. In the Housing Act of 1949, Congress defined the nation's housing goal as "the realization as soon as feasible . . . of a decent home and suitable living environment for every American family." The Act authorized construction of 810,000 units of public housing for low-income families over the next six years. But two decades after the passage of the 1949 Act, only one-half of its authorized units had been built.

In the Housing Act of 1968, Congress reiterated its determination to eliminate substandard housing, setting a ten-year deadline and an explicit goal of six million subsidized units to be provided by 1978. Unfortunately, history seems to be repeating itself, and at present rates of production for subsidized units we will be lucky to reach half of this total.

This, in itself, is not much of a justification for an expanded housing effort. Inflated promises and overambitious targets are a vagary of political life, and we are falling short of solemnly declared goals in many areas. But the targets have been much more modest and the shortfalls much greater in the housing effort. There has been no strong vested interest group to press for increased pro-

5

duction of subsidized units, since only a small number of additional families are helped by the annual production and since builders and developers have usually shied away from federal housing subsidy programs, often opposing them outright.

A second reason why increased priority should be given to housing is that it is central to the much broader problem of poverty. It is obvious that education, health, and social development suffer in the environment created by substandard and deteriorating dwellings. Though the hopes have not been fulfilled that improved housing would provide the touchstone on which all other problems would be solved, there are several practical reasons why efforts to improve the physical environment should be in the vanguard of the attack on poverty. Housing is a problem which is amenable to solution in our production oriented society. There is little doubt that we can quickly produce the necessary physical structures, at least more quickly than we can solve the intangible and intergenerational problems of poverty. The results and the costs are certainly more predictable than in other areas. And there are a number of reasons why the low-income housing problem should be attacked separately from and precedent to the income needs of the poor, beside the fact that the costs of income maintenance are staggering. There is no assurance that a guaranteed income would lead quickly to the elimination of substandard housing units. The poor might spend their money elsewhere, perhaps frivolously, and much might be siphoned off by landlords. Housing programs can guarantee that public subsidies are directed to desired ends. Most of all, they can more closely relate housing production to increased income, so that the match up between supply and demand is immediate. For these reasons, it might be better to attack the poverty problem through its components, with the provision of needed goods and services rather than the guarantee of a minimum income; certainly housing is one of the goods which should be supplied first.

Whether or not low-income housing needs are given increased priority, the current federal efforts in this area are of great importance. At present, substantially more than one million housing units are being subsidized, and several hundred thousand more are being added annually to house low-income families. In the midst of the general housing slump, the federal subsidy programs have helped to cushion the worst effects it might have had on less affluent families.

Despite the importance of these housing subsidy programs, few people are familiar with their operations. For instance, laymen often confuse the traditional FHA and VA mortgage insurance programs with those providing housing subsidies. While FHA and VA mortgage insurance are vital to many home-buyers, most of their costs are covered by premiums or small federal contributions. The degree of subsidy under these programs is not large, despite their importance, and few low-income families can take advantage of them.

Perhaps the most familiar subsidy program is public housing. Almost everyone has heard of this, usually from the horror stories of wasted money, improper management, or intolerable conditions in some projects. Not as many people are familiar with the vast contributions of this program, or with the new approaches which are improving its performance. The several private sector programs initiated in recent years are little known except by builders, developers, and others with a particular interest in low-income housing.

One reason for this confusion and general ignorance is that the subject is so complicated. There are a number of housing subsidy programs, developed through a complicated series of legislative acts, and applied with a wide range of emphasis and success. The programs cater to different groups, provide different forms of subsidy, serve different areas, and assist different types of housing. In some cases they are complementary, with several programs being used in conjunction; and in others they overlap and compete, with several providing the same type of service.

There is also a wide diversity of assistance needs. Low-income housing is needed in the central cities, in their suburbs, and in rural areas. It is needed for large families, small families, and for the elderly living alone. Some can be provided through the rehabilitation of existing units, while much requires demolition and new con-

7

struction. Subsidies must be provided for single-family ownership co-operative ownership, and for rental.

Given the diversity and complexity of the housing subsidy programs and the low-cost housing needs to which they are addressed it is little wonder that few people are familiar with all of them. Many are relatively new, so that their effectiveness is not easily measured; these have necessarily been administered by hunch as much as by conscious design. To further complicate matters, the administration of the programs was divided among a number of relatively autonomous agencies, and until a recent reorganization there was little possibility of co-ordination.

In the last few years great strides have been made toward a better understanding of low-income housing problems and programs. Two national commissions, one headed by ex-Senator Paul H. Douglas and the other by industrialist Edgar Kaiser,[4] exhaustively investigated and reported on our nation's housing. Legislation in 1968 acted on the recommendations of these commissions, creating new subsidy tools and authorizing an annual housing report covering all of the programs. An administrative reorganization within the Department of Housing and Urban Development in 1969 combined most of the subsidy programs under a single agency, laying the groundwork for improved co-ordination. And legislation in 1969 made a conscious effort to fill the gaps in existing programs and to rationalize the attack on low-income housing needs. However, much remains to be done. More data is becoming available on the newer programs, and this information must be used to measure and improve their performance. The potential for greater co-ordination must be realized through the more exact definition of the uses of the separate programs, so that they can be administered, individually and in combination, with more effectiveness. As far as possible, the housing policy should be explicitly formulated, and should aim at improving the co-ordination and operation of the separate subsidy programs.

[4] (a) National Commission on Urban Problems, *op. cit.,*
(b) President's Committee on Urban Housing, *A Decent Home* (Washington, D.C.: Government Printing Office, December 1968).

This study is an attempt to lay the groundwork for such improvements. It tries to spell out what the programs are meant to do, to measure what they have done, and to suggest what they should be doing. Special emphasis is given to their comparative and complementary features and to the more careful identification of their separate uses. This analysis is necessarily detailed and will be of greatest use to those directly concerned with the low-income housing effort. The interested layman can gain a broader understanding from the separate program analyses, but the first and last two chapters tie together the main points, outlining the programs, stressing possible improvements and priorities, and discussing the issues related to housing subsidies.

Throughout the study, housing problems and policies are discussed dispassionately and as much as possible with objectivity. The human aspects are often lost behind the cold facts and figures of program performance. Hopefully, the reader will share the underlying conviction that the housing problem of low-income families must be solved as quickly as possible, and that the human misery caused by inadequate housing is intolerable. This study focuses on solutions rather than problems, and it is intended to further the ongoing effort to improve as well as expand federal housing assistance. If even a handful of families can be rescued from a life of squalor and despair through the more efficient operation of the housing subsidy program, this attempt will have been more than justified.

2

The Legislative Origins of Housing Assistance

The legislative foundations of the housing subsidy tools are complex and can be a major source of confusion. In a number of separate housing acts over the last thirty-five years, Congress has modified and added to the assistance programs contained in a few basic pieces of legislation. The additions and modifications have been on a piecemeal basis, with too little regard for the relationship of the new or substantially modified programs to those already in existence. The result is an "alphametric soup" in which the individual programs are identified by a mixture of legislative subsections and functional labels, and in which there are few guidelines for program co-ordination. While it is difficult and often unrewarding to struggle through this legislative maze, some review is necessary if the programs are to be understood.

THE MAJOR HOUSING ACTS

The first major housing legislation was the National Housing Act of 1934, which was passed in the midst of the Depression to stimulate construction and employment, and to support the mortgage market. This Act created the Federal Housing Administration to insure long-term, low down-payment mortgages to private individuals, making homeownership possible for families of moderate income. It also established the Federal Savings and Loan Insurance Corporation, facilitating the growth of savings and loan institutions which now provide the bulk of private mortgages. Finally, the National Housing Act authorized the charter of secondary mortgage purchase associations. A single agency of this type eventually came into being—the Federal National Mortgage Association (FNMA) which provides a secondary and national market for mortgage paper, increasing the supply in areas lacking their own institutions. All of these measures were intended to increase and more equally distribute the flow of private funds into housing and to extend the possibility of homeownership to moderate income families.

The Housing Act of 1937 initiated the first true "subsidy" program—public housing. It authorized annual federal contributions to amortize the capital costs of publicly owned housing built by local agencies. The federal contribution allowed rents to be reduced so that families otherwise unable to afford adequate shelter could be properly housed. Since there was only a limited supply, public housing was usually restricted at the local level to the "depression poor"—or those with temporarily low incomes—rather than serving permanently disadvantaged families. The 1937 Housing Act also expanded slum-clearance efforts, requiring a one-to-one elimination of substandard housing for the public housing which was to be built.

Much of the public housing developed before the war was converted to military use. Afterward, veterans were given preference and with prosperity, most of the occupants increased their income with many moving on to private housing. The Veterans Administration also launched its mortgage insurance program in 1944, providing long-term home mortgages with no downpayment. These developments seemed to indicate a shift in the housing policy, with increasing emphasis on the needs of middle- and upper-income families. But in 1949 the tide suddenly reversed and the housing programs were redirected to those families with lower incomes.

12

The Housing Act of 1949 declared the national goal of a "decent home and suitable living environment for every American family." This was backed by the authorization of 135,000 units of public housing for each of the next six years, or a total of 810,000 units. Cities were given grants and loans for urban renewal, with stress on improving the total environment as well as building new housing. The 1949 legislation also initiated a separate rural housing program, to be administered by the Department of Agriculture. Since these areas could rarely carry out successful public housing developments, the Act provided for direct loans to rural individuals for the purchase or improvement of private homes.

Urban renewal and unassisted construction became the heart of the federal housing effort in the 1950's. The Housing Act of 1954 required that communities with public housing projects prepare a "workable program" for community improvement which would link public housing and renewal more closely. Grants were provided to finance the necessary planning. The 1954 Act also rechartered the FNMA, giving it special assistance funds to purchase mortgages when no private buyers could be found. These changes were not major, and the emphasis over the decade was on enlarging and perfecting the existing housing programs. Urban renewal activity was intense, and a massive volume of relatively low-cost housing was produced under the FHA and VA insurance programs, turning attention away from the housing subsidy programs. In 1959, however, a direct loan program was created providing funds to nonprofit sponsors of rental housing for the elderly. This was the first recognition of the separate and severe housing needs of the elderly, and it was also the first use of the below-market-interest rate or BMIR subsidy technique in which loans are made at less than the market rate, in this case at the lower federal borrowing rate.

In the 1960's, subsidy programs proliferated and became the center of the federal housing effort. The Housing Act of 1961 initiated assistance for families with an income too high for public housing but too low to afford adequate private shelter. Through the FNMA, the government funded BMIR loans to sponsors of

13

rental housing intended for families falling in this income gap. The interest rate was set at the federal borrowing rate, as under the 1959 loan program for housing for the elderly; and private corporations were allowed to sponsor projects as well as nonprofit groups, if they limited their profits to 6 percent.

By 1965 the cost of federal borrowing had increased to such an extent that the earlier BMIR programs lending at this rate could not provide an adequate subsidy to serve their intended clienteles. For this reason, the Housing and Urban Development Act of 1965 pegged the interest under these programs at 3 percent, and the subsidy became the difference between interest payments at this rate and those at the higher market rate. However, the 1965 Act had a more far-reaching impact, creating two major subsidy programs to be administered by the newly created Department of Housing and Urban Development (HUD). First, annual contributions were provided to local agencies for the lease of private dwellings which would be occupied by public housing tenants. Second, payments were authorized to nonprofit and limited-dividend sponsors of low-income housing; these subsidies would make up the difference between a fixed percentage of occupants' incomes and the market rents. These two programs of the 1965 Act increased the involvement of the private sector in housing lower income families, and also created an alternative to direct BMIR loans which tie up large amounts of federal funds.

The Demonstration Cities and Metropolitan Development Act of 1966 recognized that housing alone could not solve urban problems and its focus was on the whole complex of needs. However, it introduced a specific program for the rehabilitation of private housing to be sold to low-income families, providing direct loans at 3 percent interest rate. This extended the rehabilitation loan and grant programs introduced in 1964 and 1965, respectively, and for the first time subsidized home purchases by urban low-income families.

The Housing and Urban Development Act of 1968 filled out the kit of legislative tools. Like the 1965 Act, it put increasing reliance on the private sector and also sought to avoid direct federal loans

A new assistance technique was introduced—the interest subsidy payment to private financers reducing the effective interest rate paid by the nonprofit or limited-dividend sponsors of low-cost housing. Two programs were initiated which utilized this technique, one subsidizing loans to sponsors of rental housing for low-income families and the other assisting low- and moderate-income home-buyers. The 1968 Act also established the Government National Mortgage Association (GNMA) to replace the FNMA, which was made a private corporation, with the GNMA taking over its special assistance functions. The effect of this was to provide a separate source of mortgage financing for the subsidy programs and to give them a greater degree of independence from conditions in the private housing markets. Finally, the 1968 Act set a ten-year production target of 26 million housing units, including 6 million to be supplied under the subsidy programs. It directed HUD to prepare an annual housing report detailing progress toward this goal and serving as a basis for more rational legislative action.

The last and most recent legislation was the Housing and Urban Development Act of 1969. This focused on improving the programs initiated in 1968, though its major contribution was to increase public housing subsidies so as to lower the rents of its extremely low-income tenants.

The Evolution of the Present Effort

The changing thrusts and major developments in the federal housing effort can be distilled from this brief outline of housing legislation.

First, housing policy has become more explicit in its goals and more reasoned in its approach. The 1949 Housing Act first stated and quantified a national housing goal, and this was reaffirmed and requantified in the Housing and Urban Development Act of 1968. Planning has become a basic part of the housing effort, and the establishment of the Department of Housing and Urban Development in 1965 laid the groundwork for needed administrative improvements. The annual reports required by the 1968 legislation are potentially important in rationalizing congressional action.

Second, there has been an increasing emphasis on the needs of lower-income families. The subsidy programs have multiplied and expanded, increasing the housing options for low-income families. Separate sources of mortgage money have been developed for the subsidy programs, so that their operations have become more independent of conditions in the general housing markets. Most of all, the programs have been designed so that the income groups they serve span the whole range of those in need of assistance, and the subsidies have generally been increased, so that the programs can serve lower-income families.

Third, there has been an increasing reliance on the private sector. In the initial public housing program, local authorities sponsored, owned, and operated the assisted units. Later, nonprofit groups were allowed to sponsor housing projects for the elderly, and private corporations with limited profits were accepted as sponsors under other programs. Private financial institutions have an important role in the newer interest subsidy programs, and private owners and landlords are involved in the program acquiring existing units for low-income occupancy.

Finally, there has been a rapid proliferation of alternative and complementary subsidy tools. These have been added as amendments to a few major pieces of legislation and are commonly identified by either their legislative subsection or their functional title. For instance, many of the subsidy programs have been added to the National Housing Act of 1937. An amendment in 1961 initiated the Section *221(d)(3)–BMIR program*, which provided government-financed loans at a reduced rate for low-income housing development. In 1966 the *Section 221(h) program* was added, offering direct loans for the rehabilitation of private dwellings to be purchased by low-income families. And, in 1968, the Section *235* and *236* programs were introduced, with interest subsidies on mortgages for homeownership and rental housing development, respectively.

The second root legislation was the Housing Act of 1937, which initiated the *public housing program*. Public housing was given its still basic features in the 1949 Housing Act, but it has been amended several times since, most significantly in 1969. The Housing and Urban Development Act of 1965 added the Section 23 *leased housing program*, which authorizes federal contributions to local authorities for the lease of private dwellings.

The Housing Act of 1949 created the Section *502* and *504 rural loan programs*, which are administered by the Department of Agriculture, and these were augmented by the *514 farm labor housing loan*, *515 rural rental housing*, *516 farm labor housing grants*, and the *521 cooperative housing programs*. Amendments in 1965 added the Section *115 rehabilitation grant program*, which provides direct grants to homeowners in urban renewal areas. This was designed to work concurrently with the Section *312 rehabilitation loan program* of the Housing Act of 1964.

Two other pieces of legislation which contain major housing subsidy programs are: (1) the Housing Act of 1959, with its Section *202 elderly housing program*, offering BMIR loans to developers of rental housing for the elderly; and (2) the Housing and Urban Development Act of 1965 with its *rent supplement program* which provides direct payments to the sponsors of low-income housing, making up the difference between market rents and a fixed percentage of tenants' incomes.

These are the major federal subsidy programs. Others exist which involve some subsidy, but they are small or have a special and limited purpose. The following table summarizes the characteristics of the major programs in more detail, and it gives some idea of their relative contribution to the housing assistance effort. This can be used as a reference as more detailed analysis is presented.

Table 1. Summary of the major housing assistance programs

Program	Legislative origin	Assistance provided	Subsidized housing units occupied at end of fiscal 1969	Percent of 1.2 million assisted units
Public housing	Housing Act of 1937, amended many times, most notably in the Housing Act of 1949, which gave the program its present form.	Annual federal contributions to local authorities amortizing the capital costs of publicly owned housing projects. Also, supplemental federal contributions where tenant income is extremely low.	740,600	63
Leased housing	Added as Section 23 to the Housing Act of 1937 by the 1965 Housing and Urban Development Act.	Annual federal contributions to local authorities covering the difference between public housing rents and the rates paid to private owners from whom the dwelling units are leased.	44,000	4
Rent supplement	Initiated as Title I of the Housing and Urban Development Act of 1965.	Payments directly to the sponsors of low-income housing making up the difference between one-fourth of the tenants' income and market rentals.	23,000	2
236	Added as Section 236 to the National Housing Act by the Housing and Urban Development Act of 1968.	Interest subsidies to sponsors of low-income rental housing, reducing their debt payments to as low as those which would prevail at a 1% interest rate.	—	—
221(d)(3)–BMIR	Added as Section 221(d)(3) to the National Housing Act by amendment in the Housing Act	Loans are provided from GNMA special assistance funds with a BMIR of 3% to sponsors of low- and	91,000	8

Program	Origin	Description		
	of 1961, this program is to be phased out in favor of the 236 program.	moderate-income rental housing, and these interest savings permit lower rents.		
202 Elderly Housing	Initiated by the Housing Act of 1959, this program is to be phased out in favor of the 236 program.	Loans are provided directly from a revolving loan fund with a BMIR of 3% for sponsors of rental housing projects for the elderly.	26,200	2
235	Added as Section 235 to the National Housing Act by the Housing and Urban Development Act of 1968.	Interest subsidies are provided on loans to low-income families for the purchase of new, existing, or substantially rehabilitated housing. The subsidies can reduce the effective interest rate to as low as 1%.	5,500	—
221h	Added as Section 221h to the National Housing Act of 1937 by the Demonstration Cities and Metropolitan Development Act of 1966. This program is to be phased out in favor of a similar program under 235, known specifically as 235j.	Direct BMIR loans are made for the purchase and rehabilitation of dwellings for sale to low-income families. The standard rate is 3%, but this may be reduced to as low as 1% for extremely low-income families.	700	—
115 Rehabilitation Grant	Added as Section 115 of the Housing Act of 1949 by the Housing and Urban Development Act of 1965.	Grants of up to $3,500 are provided to property owners in urban renewal and code enforcement areas for the rehabilitation of housing units.	8,100	1
312 Rehabilitation Loan	Introduced as Section 312 of the Housing Act of 1964.	Direct BMIR loans at a 3% interest rate are made to homeowners and	12,500	1

Program	Legislative origin	Assistance provided	Subsidized housing units occupied at end of fiscal 1969	Percent of 1.2 million assisted units
		in some cases non-resident landlords for the rehabilitation of dwellings in urban renewal and code enforcement areas.		
502 and 504 Rural Housing Loans	Initiated under Title V of the Housing Act of 1949.	BMIR loans are provided for the purchase or improvement of rural homes, with most carrying a 5 1/8% interest rate though special credits can reduce it to as low as 1% for extremely low-income families. 1% loans are provided for minor repairs of homes owned by extremely low-income families considered ineligible for 502.	215,700	18
514 Loan and 516 Grant for Farm Labor Housing	Title V of the Housing Act of 1949.	BMIR, 5% loans are made to farm-owners, public and private groups to build or repair housing for domestic farm labor. Grants are made directly to states, localities, or broadly based nonprofit groups to build housing for domestic farm labor.	4,800	—
515 Rural Rental Housing and 521 Cooperative Housing	Title V of the Housing Act of 1949.	BMIR loans are provided to nonprofit sponsors of rental housing for low-income families in rural areas. The standard rate is 5 1/8%, but may be reduced to as low as 1% for extremely low-income families. Loans such as those under 515 are made to co-operative-owned and managed by	3,900	—

3

Public Housing

The public housing program is the cornerstone of federal housing assistance—the oldest and most widely used subsidy tool. Under this program, rental units are developed, owned, and operated by some 2,200 local authorities with subsidies from the federal government permitting rents to be reduced and low-income families to be served.

The major form of subsidy is an annual contribution to the local authority covering up to the capital costs of its public housing projects. The local authority usually finances these projects itself, selling long-term tax-free bonds in the private market, though HUD often provides short-term loans to cover construction costs and sometimes long-term loans for permanent financing. Whatever the source of capital, annual federal contributions are calculated to permit the amortization of development costs over a forty-year period, covering both debt retirement and interest expenses. In fiscal 1969 there were approximately $322 million in federal subsidies of this type.

Normally, half of the rent charged in multi-family housing goes to debt retirement and interest payments. The annual federal

21

contribution means that average public housing rentals can be reduced to around a half of market rates. Tenant payments only have to meet the remaining monthly costs—maintenance, replacement, and operating expenses. Property taxes would be an additional and substantial expense, but they are not assessed on public housing. The local government is paid 10 percent of monthly rents in their place, and this payment is less than would usually be charged. The difference is considered the local contribution to public housing costs. It is difficult to measure the amount of subsidy which comes in this form, because it varies from area to area depending on the local tax rate. A survey by the *Journal of Property Management* in 1964[1] found that in Boston, Milwaukee, Chicago, Denver, Pittsburgh, and Baltimore taxes averaged 17.5 percent of gross income from rents in apartment buildings. Since the gross income of public housing would include rents and annual contributions, the 10 percent payment in lieu of taxes is less than 5 percent of "gross income" or not even one-third of what would normally be paid in taxes. The differential is probably less in smaller cities and rural areas, but in the larger cities it is a safe estimate that public housing rents would be one-fifth more if they had to cover the full local property tax.

With annual contributions meeting capital costs and the 10 percent payment in lieu of taxes further reducing expenses, public housing rents can be substantially lower than those for private housing, but they are still often more than low-income families can afford. For this reason, additional federal subsidies are provided on public housing units occupied by especially disadvantaged families. Until 1969, supplementary annual contributions of up to $120 were provided for units occupied by elderly, displaced, extremely large or especially low-income families, if there were such a large proportion in a project that an average rent could not be charged which would cover expenses. In fiscal 1969 there were $17.8 million in supplemental annual contributions in addition to

---

[1] "Special Issue on 1964 Apartment Building Exchange," *Journal of Property Management*, Special Issue, 1964, p. 10.

he $322 million paid for the amortization of capital costs. But
ven these additional subsidies had proved insufficient in recent
ears, as operating costs increased faster than tenants' incomes.
ocal authorities were forced to raise rents, and, as a result,
any tenants had to pay an inordinately large share of their
ncome for rent. In 1967, 50 percent of all senior citizens and 22
ercent of all other families living in public housing were paying
ore than 30 percent of their income for rent.

To alleviate the burden on these families and the pressure on
cal authorities to hold down rents in the face of rising costs, the
ousing and Urban Development Act of 1969 authorized addi-
onal annual contributions to cover all rental costs in excess of
ne-fourth of tenants' incomes, less $100 deductions for children.
his will provide immediate assistance to an estimated 132,000
amilies who are paying more than 25 percent, and it may rescue
any local authorities on the brink of insolvency because of rising
osts.

With all these subsidies, the rents in public housing are extremely
w. In 1968 the median rent for families with an elderly head
as $37, and $60 for all other families. There is a wide variation
 rent since for any project the average rental is calculated to cover
perating and maintenance costs which depend on the area, the
ge of the project, and many other highly variable factors. The
ntal on any unit within a project depends on its occupant's
bility to pay. Rentals may differ on identical units, and they are
ot necessarily higher for larger units occupied by larger families.
Despite these variations there is little doubt that public housing
nts are significantly lower than the market rates on comparable
nits in the same area.

UBLIC HOUSING TENANTS

The declared purpose of public housing is to help those who
ould be otherwise ill-housed. Its subsidies are directed to families
who are in the lowest income group and who cannot afford to
ay enough to cause private enterprise in their locality or metro-

23

politan area to build an adequate supply of decent, safe, and sani
tary dwellings for their use." To assure that only such families wil
be served, income eligibility limits are set and enforced locally
These have to be approved by HUD, subject to the general rul
that they must be 20 percent below the income needed for adequat
private housing. However, approval is largely pro forma, and th
determination and application of income limits is left to loca
discretion. Because of regional variations in living and housin,
costs and in local attitudes toward who should be served, there is
wide variation in income limits. For a family of four, New Yorl
City had a maximum of $5,760 in 1967, and Chicago a maximun
of $4,600, while at the opposite extreme, Fort Worth's limit wa
only $2,700 and New Orlean's $3,000. In most cities the maximun
is between $3,500 and $4,500. The local limits are higher for large
families; for instance, in New York City they ranged from $3,88¦
for a single person to $7,896 for a family with twelve or mor
members.

With the idea that tenants should seek private housing whe
they can afford it, the local authorities also establish income maxi
mums for continued occupancy which are supposedly based on th
cost of available housing. Continued occupancy limits also var
widely; over-all, they average about 125 percent of the initia
eligibility limits. Income is re-examined every year for nonelder
families and every two years for the elderly, and except in specia
cases where no housing at reasonable rents can be found the famil
is expelled if its income is above the maximum. Of those familie
sampled in 1968, 1.89 percent were found to be overincom
and efforts were made to move them elsewhere.

Within these income limits the choice of tenants is left almos
completely to local discretion and the rules governing these choice
are only rarely made explicit. The law provides that priority shoul
be given to persons displaced by slum clearance or urban renewa
and it requires equal opportunity for Negroes; but within thes
broad guidelines local authorities devise their own rules to choos
among applicants, who in many cases greatly outnumber vacancie:
In New York City, for instance, the Douglas Commission foun

762 applications for every vacancy in its 1968 investigation, and 126 in Chicago. Some rationing method is obviously needed. Local authorities usually create their own standards to select the most "desirable" tenants, and these have drawn criticism in a number of cases. Discrimination against Negroes, addicts, and even prostitutes has been decried by civil liberties groups; while at the opposite extreme, tenant organizations have often demanded stricter selection standards to keep out the "riff-raff."

Without question, however, the public housing program is serving a low-income and seriously disadvantaged clientele which would otherwise be ill-housed. Overwhelmingly, its tenants are poor and dependent on transfer payments for a large portion of their income. The following data are for tenants re-examined in the first nine months of 1968.

Table 2. Selected characteristics of public housing tenants re-examined in the first nine months of 1968

	Nonelderly head	Elderly head
Percent of re-examined	67.8%	32.2%
Average no. of persons	4.5	1.8
Gross income		
Less than $1,000	2%	11%
$1,000–1,499	6	33
$1,500–1,999	10	19
$2,000–2,499	10	13
$2,500–2,999	10	8
$3,000–3,499	11	5
$3,500–3,999	10	3
$4,000–4,499	8	2
$4,500–4,999	7	2
$5,000–5,999	10	1
$6,000–6,999	6	—
$7,000–7,999	8	—
More than $8,000	1	—
Median	$3,532	$1,656
Receiving assistance or benefits	40%	95%

SOURCE: HAA Statistics, Department of Housing and Urban Development.

25

PRODUCTION OF PUBLIC HOUSING

With the administration of public housing left to local authorities under broad guidelines, federal efforts concentrate on the production of new units. Federal policy largely determines the quantity, distribution, and quality of new public housing. Most visibly authorizations for new contractual commitments govern the amount of new construction which can be undertaken by local authorities. These authorizations have fluctuated markedly over the years as support has waxed and waned; and as a result, there have been large variations in annual public housing starts as shown in the following plot of aggregate figures (Chart I). At the local and regional levels, the variation is even more marked. But despite these fluctuations the public housing stock has constantly increased until there were 740,580 publicly owned units under management at the end of fiscal 1969 (not including those developed for leasing). In that year, 65,300 more were started, which is nearly as many as under the rest of HUD's assistance programs combined. The public housing program still remains the primary tool for producing low-cost housing.

EQUIVALENT ELIMINATION

Public housing production is governed by two important legislative provisions. First, the Housing Act of 1949 requires that for every public housing unit which is built, a substandard or unsafe dwelling unit must be eliminated within five years through demolition, condemnation, or effective closing. This "equivalent elimination" provision may be deferred in localities with acute shortages of decent and safe low-cost housing, but the thrust is that the program should upgrade the housing stock rather than add to it. Under the urban renewal program, a large number of dwellings occupied by low-income families have been torn down and replaced for the most part by nonresidential or luxury apartment buildings. The Douglas Commission estimated that there has been a net loss of 400,000 low-income units under urban renewal, and most of these

26

CHART 1

PUBLIC HOUSING
NEW CONSTRUCTION AND REHABILITATION STARTS
BY YEAR

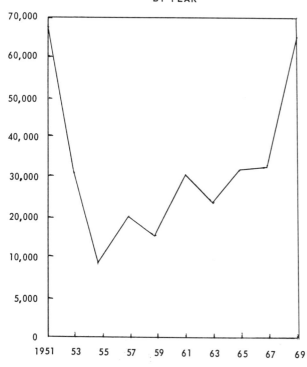

Source: HAA Statistics, Department of Housing and Urban Development

represent "equivalently eliminated" units offsetting a large portion of the more than 700,000 public housing units produced. The Housing and Urban Development Act of 1969 removed the additional requirement that local authorities prepare a "workable program" which, among other things, explicitly correlated clearance

27

and construction. How this change, and the current housing shortages, will affect HUD's policy toward equivalent elimination remains to be seen.

DEVELOPMENT COST LIMITS

A second set of legislative regulations which have greatly influenced the distribution and quality of public housing starts are their development cost limits. These were changed by the Housing and Urban Development Act of 1969 from $2,400 for units designed for the nonelderly and $3,500 on those for elderly, to $2,800 and $4,000, respectively. The special allowance of $750 above the regular limits for high-cost areas was raised to $1,500.

The earlier and lower cost limits had become one of the major determinants of the distribution of starts. Due to rapidly increasing costs, the limits were too low for most cities. Public housing was forced into the low-cost regions and smaller cities. At the end of 1967 cities under 100,000 had 41 percent of all public housing units, but by the end of 1968 their share increased to 44 percent. The twenty largest cities had 34.3 percent of all units under management as of September 30, 1967, but only 30.1 percent of those under management at the close of 1969.

The structure of the cost limits also distorted the type of housing which was built. The higher limit on housing for the elderly was much larger than any real cost differential, and many areas found that only housing for the elderly could be built for less than the limits. This added to the fact that housing for the elderly usually faces less neighborhood opposition and is easier to develop. As a result, the percentage of starts intended for housing the elderly increased steadily from 25.6 percent in 1964 to 33.6 percent in 1967 and 41.2 percent in fiscal 1969.

Revisions of the cost limits in 1969 were meant to alleviate these distortions. The limits for housing the nonelderly were increased more than those for housing the elderly; and the high-cost area limits were increased more than the regular limits. Marginally, the effect will be to increase the proportion of starts

28

which are possible in higher-cost areas and those for housing for the nonelderly. But this will not correct the situation permanently, since costs will rise and catch up with the higher limits. What is needed is a formula based on local, private development costs, as is contained in the Administration's 1970 legislative proposal. Any simple legislatively determined cost limits will be selectively limiting if they are limiting at all; their effect will be to distort the distribution and types of public housing starts.

METHODS OF DEVELOPING PUBLIC HOUSING

Federal concern with public housing costs had led to the adoption of new and hopefully less expensive development methods. The conventional production method is for the local authority to draw up a set of preliminary designs and standards, and after approval by HUD to submit these to competitive bidding. The lowest bidder then builds the project, with the local authority ordinarily providing construction financing, usually through the sale of short-term notes in the private market. The authority "owns" the project from its inception, and the builder works under normal bid-contract procedures.

Though this development method results in the cost savings of competition, there are often so few bidders that the economies from competition are more theoretical than real. And the time involved in setting up initial designs, submitting these for bid, and selecting the developer, can be lengthy and costly. The Douglas Commission found that in 1967 the average time from application to the beginning of site preparation was nearly a year in public housing. Changes were made in 1968 to cut this time to eighty-five working days, but an alternative development method was also adopted on a larger scale—turnkey construction.

The turnkey method is different from the conventional approach in that the developer builds on land he owns, with payment on completion when he "turns over the keys" to the local authority. The final price and broad specifications are stated in the initial contract; but there is no detailed project approval and no competitive bid, which saves time. Since financing during the construction period is handled by the builder, he finds it to his advantage to proceed as fast as possible, and this can lead to further time and cost savings.

The performance of the turnkey procedure, which was first used on an experimental basis in January 1966, has generally been favorable. Aggregate cost comparisons understate the relative effectiveness of turnkey, since its projects have been concentrated in high-cost urban areas. But in the second half of fiscal 1968, total development costs per room on conventional projects throughout the country were 17 percent more than on turnkey projects. On a per-unit basis, the differential was slightly less, but only because turnkey units had 4.66 rooms on the average compared to 3.98 for conventional units. For units accepted during fiscal 1969, total development costs per unit and room on conventional projections were, respectively, 2 and 1 percent more. Careful time comparisons have not been made between turnkey and conventional methods since the latter have been improved, but HUD officials feel that the difference is significant.

Because of these advantages, turnkey has become the primary method of developing public housing. Though most authorities still use conventional methods, the minority using turnkey extensively are by far the more active ones; and of all the units accepted in fiscal 1969, 29,476 were turnkey while only 18,438 were conventional.

Another method of public housing development is through direct acquisition. Local authorities can purchase housing directly from the existing stock, and these units can be occupied with or without rehabilitation. Such acquisitions accounted for 15 percent of acceptances in fiscal 1969. Costs under this method are not comparable with those under the turnkey or conventional methods, since the housing is older, a great deal is rehabilitated, and the houses usually have more rooms and serve larger families. However, it is clearly cheaper to provide a given number of housing units through acquisition than through new construction, as seen in Table 3.

30

Table 3. Selected characteristics of public housing units accepted in fiscal 1969, by type

Type of program	Number of projects	Number of units	Percent of all units	Average number of units per project	Average number of rooms per unit	Average TDC per unit	Average TDC per room
All programs (except leased), total*	540	58,863	100%	109	4.28	$16,246	$3,794
All elderly	196	22,298	38	114	3.23	15,618	4,839
None elderly	216	24,382	41	113	4.22	16,400	3,143
Mixed	128	12,183	21	95	4.34	17,086	3,937
Conventional, new, total	178	18,438	31	104	4.21	17,270	4,101
Turnkey, new, total	268	29,476	50	110	4.17	16,909	4,050
Turnkey, rehab, total	9	838	1	93	4.42	14,137	3,198
Acquisition with rehab, total	10	5,798	10	58	4.50	11,353	2,525
Acquisition without rehab, total	34	3,081	5	91	4.74	14,844	3,129

* There are 41 projects for Indians, accounting for 1,231 accepted units which are included in this total but not in the separate categories.
SOURCE: HAA Statistics' Department of Housing and Urban Development.

FISCAL DIFFICULTIES IN PUBLIC HOUSING

Though public housing is the oldest, largest, and currently most important subsidy program, it is beset by problems hindering its performance. Until 1969 the most critical of these was its difficulty in continuing to serve the lowest income families. With subsidies tied to capital costs, increases in operating and maintenance expenses demanded increased rents; such expenses have been rising faster than the income and rent-paying ability of tenants. In New York City tenant income increased 65.1 percent between 1952 and 1967, while routine operating expenses increased 125.6 percent. Detroit had an even worse experience, with operating expenses increasing 106 percent compared to a 9 percent increase in tenant income. If rents were raised by less than the cost increases, the local authority would have to dig into its reserves for replacements and repairs. Most authorities chose this course, drawing down reserves rather than fully increasing rents. In New York City, for instance, rents were raised only 71.6 percent, despite expense increases of 125.6 percent between 1952 and 1967. But reserves were gradually depleted, and more and more local authorities were experiencing grave financial difficulties. HUD surveyed eighty major housing authorities in 1968, which accounted for almost two-thirds of all public housing units. It found that thirty-nine were operating at a deficit, while fifty-one were receiving insufficient income from rents to meet nonroutine needs such as replacement and extraordinary repairs. Fifteen authorities, including those in seven of the ten largest cities, were at the point of insolvency.[2] Conditions were indeed desperate.

To solve these problems, the Housing and Urban Development Act of 1969 provides for direct contributions to local authorities, making up the difference between rents and what occupants can pay with one-fourth of their income. This measure, if implemented, would relieve the pressure on local authorities, allowing them to

[2] "Necessity for Rental Assistance to Very Low-Income Tenants of Public Housing Projects," *Congressional Record—House,* November 13, 1969, H10863.

32

raise rents to cover their full operating expenses a
much needed repairs and replacement. It would
financial burdens of the estimated 132,000 familie
in public housing but are paying more than 25 ⌐
income in rent. And these short-run effects miჯ
significant than the longer-run impact. Public housing would now
be opened to the lowest-income families, since there would be no
minimum to be paid, and local authorities would have no reason
to reject the poorest of the poor because of doubts of their rent-
paying ability.

THE QUALITY OF PUBLIC HOUSING

Perhaps the most critical unresolved issues center on the qualitative aspects of public housing. Six of the eight specific criticisms of
the program by the Douglas Commission were directed at such
problems.

Summarizing, we consider the chief weaknesses of public housing
to be the following:

. . . .

(2) A failure to take advantage of cost reduction methods of construction which could be carried out without any real loss in quality . . .

(3) A failure to coordinate the minimum required standards for
public housing with those for FHA housing.

(4) A pronounced tendency to build an excessive number of extremely high-rise and closely massed apartments, which make a
better communal life very difficult and which identify the occupants
as dwellers in "poor town."

(5) A comparative disregard of the needs of children and of
large families through an undue concentration on apartments having
two bedrooms or less . . .

(6) A comparative neglect of the services that the occupants and
those in the surrounding community need and that are essential to
modern city life.

(7) A comparative neglect of the importance of design and beauty,
which are elements in the good life along with space, light and
shelter.[3]

[3] National Commission on Urban Problems, *Building the American City*
(Washington, D.C.: Government Printing Office, 1969), p. 119.

All of these problems cannot be solved immediately; and in some ways, their solutions may be mutually exclusive. For instance, cost considerations conflict with the goal of dispersing public housing, since there is good evidence that large, multi-building projects can be substantially cheaper than those built on scattered sites. The problems also involve normative issues which will be difficult to resolve. For example, increased assistance for large families is needed, but similar "needs" arguments can be raised for other groups. The fact that proportionately more large families remain to be housed does not detract from the benefits received by those in other groups who are housed.

Another imponderable question is that of amenities in public housing, especially when the opportunity costs of these amenities are calculated in terms of standard units of adequate shelter for those who are not being served. While the normative issues must be resolved elsewhere, it is worth noting that the marginal cost of such amenities may not be large. In a study of project costs in New York City, estimates were made of "basic housing costs" on a number of projects, subtracting the cost of every unnecessary item or special feature. For public housing projects these nonessential items amounted to only 3 percent of development costs. But on unassisted FHA projects they were still only 11 percent, and even in luxury apartments in Manhattan they accounted for only 14 percent of total costs.[4] This indicates that the price of luxury may not be large. Whatever the cost, however, the public is not likely to approve of luxury appointments for public housing, and the question of amenities will continue to be controversial.

With the increased subsidies initiated in 1969 providing coverage of full operating costs, local authorities should have the means, which may or may not be used, to improve their maintenance and care of public housing. And federal guidelines for these subsidies require "satisfactory standards of management and tenant respon-

[4] Department of Housing and Urban Development, *Cost and Time Associated with New Multifamily Housing Construction in New York City* (Washington, D.C.: Government Printing Office, 1969).

sibility." This may result in the alleviation of many of the problems which have resulted in rent strikes around the country, most notably in St. Louis. But the causes of discontent go deeper than rent levels and the quality of maintenance, and these may be exacerbated by changes in the subsidy formula. Attempts by local authorities to increase the number of lower-income families in their projects may be resisted by tenants. No matter what the income class, there seems to be a strong repulsion towards families of lower income; attempts to mix different income groups, even in subsidized housing, have had little success. There is a movement which has surfaced in New York and Boston to give greater powers over admission to tenant committees, and if this occurs, poorer families may be excluded. Whether local authorities bend to this pressure, and whether, indeed, it becomes significant, provision will have to be made for substantial increases in management and special services if the poorest of the poor are moved into public housing projects on a large scale.

LOCAL AUTHORITY ADMINISTRATION

Most of these normative issues must be resolved at the federal level, but many policy decisions, and certainly their implementation, will be the responsibility of the local authorities. Unfortunately, there are serious questions about the ability of many authorities to carry out desired reforms, to expand their efforts, and to adapt them to changing needs and conditions. In April 1968 there were 2,156 local authorities administering public housing projects. Thirty percent of these had less than 50 units, 50 percent had less than 100 units, and only 14 percent had over 500 units, though the largest authorities contained the majority of units. Smaller authorities can rarely afford the highly trained staffs needed to develop and operate public housing effectively, and the majority depend almost entirely on the abilities of inexperienced and part-time citizens serving on their boards. Even if a permanent staff exists, policy matters are decided by the board. Typically, this consists of five members appointed by the mayor or

35

county board of supervisors for four- to five-year terms. There are no qualifications for membership and there is usually no compensation. The local authority is thus constituted as an independent and supposedly apolitical agency, with "outstanding private citizens" serving on its board.

A survey of 1,891 board members in 1968 found that they were overwhelmingly business executives, lawyers, real estate men, and bankers. In authorities operating 1,000 units, 90 percent were male, 89 percent were white, and the median income was well over $20,000, with less than 5 percent earning under $5,000.[5] Obviously, these are "outstanding" private citizens, but it is questionable whether they can devote the necessary time to complex public housing matters and whether they can understand and adapt to the changing needs which public housing must meet.

As the program increasingly is called upon to serve the needs of the "permanent poor," and as the life style and interests of the program's clientele and its governors increasingly diverge, the original concept of the housing authority becomes less and less adequate. It may be asked whether a group which is so completely unrepresentative in basic demographic terms of the clientele it serves can adequately understand, sympathize with, serve and protect that clientele.[6]

The response of board members to an opinion sampling substantiated this point. Asked why they were not adding any more public housing, the members most often replied that the housing authority itself felt that there was enough. Only rarely cited was the lack of federal funds. Of those sampled, over 57 percent agreed and only 27 percent disagreed with the statement that "at present the authority needs stricter rules and regulations, and proper means of enforcing them, in order to promote acceptable behavior." Only 24 percent felt that authorities ought to recognize tenant unions; while less than half disagreed with the statement that

[5] Chester W. Hartmann and Gregg Carr, "Housing Authorities Reconsidered," *Journal of the American Institute of Planners*, vol. XXXV, no. 1 (January 1969): 12.

[6] *Ibid.*, p. 13.

"most public housing tenants have no initiative."[7] The increasing demands of tenant groups seem foreboding when contrasted with these attitudes, and the potential for conflict is obvious.

One solution to the weaknesses of local authorities is to shift responsibility elsewhere. This is the essence of the turnkey construction method, and of various other experimental programs such as Turnkey II, where local authorities hire private management firms, and Turnkey III, in which the public housing units are gradually sold to tenants. Under these methods, the local authority's operational responsibility and control are reduced. Unfortunately, the authorities who are least capable and least active are rarely the ones who use such techniques. As the following chart shows, it is the larger authorities who are using the newer methods, though even among these the alternative approaches must become more widespread before all will benefit from the options they offer.

A more direct approach to public housing's organizational problems is to improve the quality of local authorities. This can be done by creating full-time, well-paid boards. For instance, New York City recently created a three-member board whose chairman is paid $35,000 and the other two members $25,000 annually. This could be done in the other large authorities, but it is not feasible in the smaller ones. These might be improved by closer links with local governments.

But there is clearly a need for stricter federal guidelines and more active involvement of the federal government where local authorities fall short. Funds can be tied to reforms, as is the case with modernization grants which require tenant participation in decisions. Potentially, the greatest source of control is the supplemental annual contribution for extremely low-income tenants, with its requirement that local authorities meet some as yet unspecified standards. Stricter guidelines should be created by Congress and enforced by HUD. Almost all authorities can be expected to comply in order to get the much needed funds.

[7] *Ibid.*, p. 16.

Table 4.   Use of innovative public housing approaches by local authorities

	Authorities with over 1,000 units		All authorities	
	Use	Plan to use	Use	Plan to use
Turnkey	11%	33%	4%	12%
Rehabilitation	15	21	4	9
Mixed public and private sponsors	5	27	3	9
Scattered-site construction	24	28	18	20

SOURCE: Chester W. Hartmann and Gregg Carr, "Housing Authorities Reconsidered," *Journal of American Institute of Planners*, vol. XXXV (January 1969).

THE ROLE OF PUBLIC HOUSING

Despite these problems, public housing must continue to be the primary subsidy tool. The program has several important and distinctive features which set it apart from the other assistance programs, differences which will become clear as these other efforts are analyzed. First, the dwellings are owned and operated by public authorities. The "public" has control over and responsibility for maintenance, operation, tenant selection, and rent determination to a greater degree than under any other assistance program, and it has a stock of housing units permanently available for low-income use. Second, in public housing, there is more control over the cost, design, and quality of the assisted housing; as a purchaser rather than a subsidizer, the government has more leverage, though this has rarely been exerted in practice. Third, the public housing program, both by design and default, has come to serve the lowest-income families; only the much smaller rent supplement program among the other assistance tools reaches so low. Having assumed this role, the level of public housing activity largely determines whether the needs of the poor are met.

There is little argument that these characteristics of public housing make it fundamental in the housing strategy. While many problems require alternative approaches, and can be solved by subsidies to the private sector with smaller levels of assistance, the needs of perhaps a majority of ill-housed, poor, and elderly families can only be met through the active involvement of the government and with substantial subsidies.

This greater involvement is hardly beneficial if public decisions are not "good," which is too often the case, especially at the local level. Administrative improvements must be carried out before the public housing program will operate most effectively and will be able to resolve the highly volatile issues lurking ahead—the degree of tenant control, the extent of services and amenities in public housing, and the clientele which it will serve. But even as it is presently constituted, public housing does much which the programs oriented to the private sector cannot do. Though some things are done wrong, public housing builds for and shelters the lowest-income and most disadvantaged clientele, and it is absolutely necessary if their vast needs are to be met.

4

Leased Housing

The leased housing program has many obvious similarities with public housing. It is authorized under the Housing Act of 1937 and is legislatively a public housing program; it is funded out of public housing appropriations; and it is administered through the local authorities using many public housing procedures. But there are also very significant differences. Leased housing is privately not publicly owned, and it may be existing as well as new. Leased units are more easily dispersed throughout the community and do not necessarily carry the stigma of public housing. They may more effectively serve certain groups among the public housing clientele, and their subsidy may differ. With these, and other distinctive features, the leasing program should be distinguished from the other forms of public housing discussed in the preceding chapter. Though it has rarely gained separate recognition and consideration, it has a separate role to play in the housing effort.

PROGRAM DESIGN

Under the leasing program, local public housing authorities lease privately owned dwelling units for occupancy by low-income tenants. The housing may be of any type—single-family or row houses, mobile homes, or multi-family units—and it may be new, substantially rehabilitated or as is. Local authorities are directed to avoid slum and central city locations, with the hope of dispersing leased units. There is a legislative guideline stating that no more than 10 percent of the units in any particular project are to be leased. This can be, and usually is, waived by the local authority, but it expresses the legislative intent that leased housing should not take on project proportions and should be scattered throughout the community.

The way leasing works is that renewable contracts are made, running for up to five years, which commit the local authority to the continued rental of a stated number of privately owned units at a specified rent. The rental paid to the property owner may not exceed the local market rate on a comparable unit. Owner responsibilities and the rules governing the tenant-owner and owner-authority relationships are spelled out in this contract. The owner can bargain for choice of tenants, or may accept assignment by the authority; most leave it to the local authority, since if they choose the tenants they are also responsible for any vacancy losses.

Leased housing tenants are usually chosen from among those eligible for public housing, although the local authority may and sometimes does establish separate and higher income limits under the leasing program, where these may be necessary to bring in tenants who are acceptable to the private owners. In leased housing there are no income limits for continued occupancy. If the tenant raises his income past the local public housing maximum, he may continue to live in the unit, paying market rates and receiving no subsidy. The hope is that families with increasing income will remain in their leased units, setting an example for other subsidized tenants and becoming truly integrated into the community in which they live.

Assistance under the leasing program is provided through an annual federal contribution to the local authority. This makes up the difference between the normal public housing rents which are usually charged and the amount paid to the property owner under the lease agreement. The maximum federal contribution is based

42

on the local cost of developing new public housing of comparable unit size; it is computed as the annual amount which would amortize this cost at current interest rates for local authority borrowing. Additional contributions are made, as under public housing, if the tenant has an extremely low income.

The subsidy under this formula can be no larger than on a unit of new public housing of comparable size. Hopefully, it will be less. If the leased unit is older, its market rent will probably be less than the total annual costs of a new unit of public housing. Since contracted rent under the leasing agreement cannot exceed the market rate, and since the tenant pays at least the public housing rent, the federal subsidy should not be as large as that of a comparable public housing unit.

The Potential Benefits of Leasing

If the program works as it is designed, everyone benefits from leasing. The owner of the dwelling, while receiving no more than the market rent, has a long-term guarantee of occupancy and rent payments. This is no small matter. For the country as a whole in 1966, losses in income due to vacancies and delinquent rents were between 3.5 and 5 percent of gross possible income on rental projects. For low-income housing, the losses are several times this amount, and increased income of 10 to 15 percent may not be unlikely as a result of the leasing guarantee. Of course, the local authority negotiates to get some of this savings, and tries to lease units at less than the market rate, but the property owners are likely to profit.

The government benefits from this arrangement, since, theoretically, the low-income families are housed for less or at least no more than it would cost in new public housing. Other goals are possibly achieved, such as the penetration of more affluent neighborhoods, a mix of subsidized and unsubsidized units, and a greater use of the housing stock.

But, most significantly, the tenants of leased housing can benefit. The maximum federal contribution is the amount which would be

43

paid on a new public housing unit with an equal number of bedrooms. Older units of any size are likely to cost less, unless they have other, better features. With the difference in "per-bedroom" price, the local authority can afford more of these other features. Though the leased housing tenant is paying the same or slightly more rent than he would in public housing, he is getting better housing and supposedly a better location. Hopefully, he will escape the stigma of public housing occupancy.

The potential benefits of leasing are not as clearcut when new rather than existing dwellings are leased. The only ones who are sure to profit are the developers and owners. They have a guaranteed cash flow which increases their annual earnings and makes leasing more attractive than competitive rental. Equity is built up in the unit, accelerated tax depreciation is allowed, and if development and operating costs are less than those under public housing, there can be extra earnings. All these can make leasing more attractive than turnkey sale to the local authority, and there is little doubt that developers and owners will find the leasing program extremely attractive.

There seem to be few advantages to the government in leasing rather than purchasing new housing. Cases of temporary demand are rare and can be filled through the lease of existing units in most conceivable instances. The short-term nature of the lease will probably work in one direction only. While the owner may terminate the lease if he finds a more profitable use for his property, it is difficult to imagine the local authority uprooting the tenants of a leased dwelling because of better lease terms elsewhere. Localities may find leasing attractive because it permits taxation which will yield more than the 10 percent payment under public housing, but the federal revenue loss is many times greater because of the income tax shelter provided. The one possible advantage is the case where developers would not build under turnkey, though they will do so with a lease guarantee. How often this may be the case is not known.

The major shortcoming is that the benefits to tenants are likely to be much less. Newly constructed units differ little from regular public housing. They are built with the same cost limits, since maximum contributions are calculated on the basis of units developed under these limits. Private owners and developers are likely to cut as many costs as possible in construction and operation in order to increase their profits, and this may result in lesser quality as well as greater economy. There is no reason to expect an income mix in projects built largely for public housing tenants, and there is no reason to expect that communities will accept them more willingly because they are leased rather than publicly owned. Projects developed for leasing and occupancy by public housing tenants should have no more success in penetrating affluent neighborhoods than those developed through turnkey methods.

THE PERFORMANCE OF THE LEASING PROGRAM

These theoretical considerations reveal little about the actual performance of the leased housing program. Unfortunately, data is limited; and it is difficult to determine whether leasing has realized its objectives. The characteristics of leased units and their occupants can only be pieced together from a variety of sources.

Case studies have yielded some fragmentary evidence.[1] For example, in some cities, a large proportion of leased housing units are occupied by former tenants. Half of a sampling of tenants in Chicago had already lived in these units before they were leased, which meant that there was no dispersion of these families and that leasing was close to a direct housing subsidy. Chicago has an unusually high percentage, however, and the 20 percent proportion of Oklahoma City is probably more typical. In some cities authorities impose arbitrary rules on the units which will be leased. New York City will not lease any units in slum areas unless renewal is substantially completed, while Washington, D.C., requires amenities, such as a fenced-in lawn and proximity to community

---

[1] Lawrence M. Friedman and James E. Krier, "A New Lease On Life: Section 23 Housing and the Poor," *University of Pennsylvania Law Review*, vol. 116, no. 4 (February 1968).

45

facilities, before it will lease. Other authorities have special rules for tenant selection, under the assumption that only the "rich poor" and the more "socially acceptable" families can be integrated into more affluent communities. Income limits and rents are raised in some cases; while in others qualitative standards are introduced. In Washington, D.C., less than 10 percent of the first 139 families placed in leased units were headed by women. Many authorities concentrate on leasing for the elderly, since they are usually more "acceptable" than other low-income households.

However, it is dangerous to generalize on these examples, and directly opposite cases can be found in each instance. Washington, D.C., and Boston have only a very small proportion of leased housing units occupied by previous tenants; 70 percent of the tenant families in Oklahoma City were headed by females; and some authorities, such as in Omaha, Nebraska, use the leasing program mostly for large families rather than for the elderly.

The following characteristics were calculated from the records of 864 leased housing occupants in the New York region, for whom information was available as of March 31, 1969. These are compared with the characteristics of public housing tenants re-examined in the same region during the first nine months of 1968, and those who moved during that period. On the basis of this limited evidence, one might conclude that leased housing tenants are not very different from those already located in regular public housing, but that they have larger families and are slightly better-off than those who are presently moving in. The rents in leased housing are higher. The New York region may not be typical, however, and these observations are only tentative, pointing to the need for more careful and complete statistical analysis of the leased housing program.

This need is especially critical in light of HUD estimates of subsidies under public housing and leasing. Their estimates, shown in Table 6, suggest that leased housing subsidies are more and not less than those under new conventional and turnkey public housing. This might be expected if leased units were larger on the average, or had more low-income families receiving supple-

Table 5. Characteristics of leased housing tenants compared to those in all public housing, New York region

Incomes	Leased	In public housing	Moving in
Less than $1,000	1%	2%	3%
$1,000–1,999	20	18	22
$2,000–2,999	27	17	24
$3,000–3,999	22	14	18
$4,000–4,999	17	14	16
$5,000–5,999	7	12	9
$6,000–6,999	4	8	5
More than $7,000	2	12	3
Average persons	3.29	3.48	2.86
Percent with more than five	25%	29%	17%
Average gross rent	$69	$66	$57

SOURCE: HAA Statistics, Department of Housing and Urban Development.

mental contributions, but it is not clear that either is the case. Leased housing units in the New York region were found to have fewer occupants per unit than the public housing average, though more than those occupied by families moving into what may or may not be new units. But supplemental contributions under the leasing program in fiscal 1969 were only .2 percent of annual contributions compared with 4.9 percent under the other public housing programs. This suggests, though it in no sense proves, that rental contracts are very liberal. The private owners leasing to local authorities are apparently making out well in their bargaining and the potential savings of leasing are perhaps not being realized. Certainly, further examination is needed of the clientele of leased housing and of the comparable costs of leasing.

Table 6. Average subsidies for units under payment

	1968 actual	1969 estimate	1970 estimate
Conventional new	$708	$745	$790
Turnkey new	822	687	769
Leased housing	779	805	820

SOURCE: Department of Housing and Urban Development.

Whatever its costs or qualitative achievements, there is little debate that leasing has effectively housed a large number of low-income families in a short time. Through fiscal 1969, a cumulative total of 94,291 units had been accepted or, in other words, local authorities had contract authority for that number of units, and by December 31, 1969, there were 54,304 units of leased housing available for occupancy. In the first half of fiscal 1970, acceptances were executed for 12,757 leased units compared with 28,599 under the other public housing programs.

These aggregate figures conceal some interesting facts. While many housing units have been leased, only a small percentage of all authorities have participated in the program, and the majority of units are concentrated among an even smaller proportion of these. At the end of 1969 less than 20 percent of all authorities had leasing projects and almost half of those who did were leasing less than 100 units. Only 3 percent of all authorities had more than 500 leased units, but they accounted for 60 percent of the total acceptances. The active participants include some of the largest cities, such as Chicago, Boston, Los Angeles, New York, Philadelphia, San Francisco, Atlanta, and Minneapolis. Authorities in the Pacific states have participated much more heavily, so that the San Francisco public housing region, one of six national regions, accounted for 34 percent of all leased units accepted through fiscal 1969. There, as in the New York region, the active authorities shifted emphasis from the other forms of public housing, with leasing currently accounting for more acceptances than the other public housing programs. Over-all, in the first half of fiscal 1970 leased acceptances were 45 percent of those under the other public housing programs.

Leasing New Versus Old Units

Increasingly, leased units are new rather than existing. Of those units available for occupancy at the end of fiscal 1969, only 7 percent had been newly constructed, while 69 percent were unrehabili-tated existing units. More than half of all contract commitments made in the first half of fiscal 1970 provided for newly constructed units, and only 29 percent were for unrehabilitated dwellings. There has been a very definite change of policy, with the production division of HUD targetting a 48 percent acceptance of new units in fiscal 1970 and only 38 percent of existing units.

This emphasis on newly constructed units is at variance with the original legislation, which conceived of leasing as a way to take "full advantage of vacancies or potential vacancies in the private housing market" to provide "low-rent housing in private accommodations" or "dwelling units in an existing structure." There can be little doubt that this meant older units and not those built for leasing. The law in fact prohibits HUD from making specific contractual commitments until the housing is completed and thus "existing"; without this prior commitment, few developers would undertake a low-income project.

The change in policy has been administrative rather than legislative. HUD argues that the Housing and Urban Development Act of 1968, with its focus on housing production, reversed the original congressional intent. HUD claims that because the lease of a pre-existing dwelling does not add to the housing stock, leased units cannot be included in production figures and leasing is therefore unwarranted. Whatever the validity of this argument, HUD can lease any proportion of new units it chooses, as long as it does not make precommitments for leasing.

The restriction on precommitments is circumvented by the fact that local authorities can and do make prior guarantees to developers. The authority receives a federal contribution commitment for a specified number of leased units of designated sizes. This is a "hunting license" authorizing lease agreements which the local authority makes at its discretion. Portions can be reserved for units yet to be built, though no contributions will be paid until the project is completed. This ties up contract authority and leaves it unused, but it is a necessary sleight of hand if units are to be built for leasing, since most developers require a prior commitment.

The real issue is whether the decision to emphasize new construction is wise. Where a large number of vacancies exist, the lease of existing units will more effectively utilize the housing stock and will more quickly and cheaply house low-income families than new construction. But housing markets are tight and vacancy rates are rock bottom. HUD's guidelines for leasing dictate that where the vacancy rate is less than 3 percent for any size unit the local authority should stress new construction or substantial rehabilitation to avoid inflationary effects. Vacancy rates in almost all cities are less than 3 percent, which would seem a justification for the change in policy toward new construction. There are, however, several important reservations.

First, the vacancy-rate statistics hide the fact that there is usually a concentration of vacancies in certain areas of most larger cities. These are often in run-down neighborhoods where location is undesirable; but they may also be in better areas, especially those in the process of racial transition. Even if these vacancies are in less desirable locations the units may be standard and of better quality than those presently occupied by the ill-housed. Where leasing will put better quality housing to use, and will reduce the housing expenses of low-income families, it may be justified.

Second, vacancies in many areas are self-generating, where vandals move in the minute more than a few units are empty. Owners are unwilling to make improvements because they justifiably fear that they could not find tenants for improved buildings. In the larger cities there are a vast number of dwellings which are not substandard or which could easily be rehabilitated, yet they are abandoned by their owners. In Detroit there are 3,000 empty buildings; in Boston the number has increased from 450 to 800 in the last year; in Philadelphia there are an estimated 24,000 vacant residential structures and 7,500 in Houston; in New York City 114,000 apartments have been lost since 1965 because of abandonment.[2] Certainly, the majority of these cannot or should not be saved, but many could be rehabilitated and some occupied as is, with lease guarantees; also, units which would otherwise be

[2] John Herbers, "Urban Paradox: Dwellings Abandoned Despite Housing Shortage," *New York Times*, February 9, 1970, p. 39.

abandoned in the future can be saved. This would involve a different emphasis in the leasing program, but it is one which should be seriously considered, based on its potential benefits.

Third, the inflationary effects of the leasing program are likely to be minimal. The relationship between declining vacancy rates and increasing prices has not been measured; but the leasing program is unlikely to have a great effect, since it will provide only a small number of units in any particular area given current program levels. Those cities with the largest number of leased units have reported no special inflation of housing costs; if other cities with similar conditions participated equally, aggregate leasing activity could be expanded severalfold. And the leasing program is self-limiting. If no vacancies existed, the private owner would not lease his property for low-income occupancy, since he could easily find higher quality tenants and vacancy losses would be low. No shortage has as yet been reported in the number of dwellings available for lease.

These considerations would suggest that the lease of existing or rehabilitated dwellings should not be de-emphasized. This, in fact, should be the primary purpose of leasing, as was the original congressional intent. New construction can better be handled under the public housing methods, where the government gets more for its money in terms of equity build-up and control. If the leases of existing units are unfeasible, the program as a whole should receive less priority rather than its being used for a purpose where it is not as effective as other tools. New Units should not be leased unless leasing is more expedient than turnkey purchase, which will rarely be the case.

5

Rent Supplements

As its name implies, the rent supplement program subsidizes the rental payments of low-income families. Government contributions make up the difference between market rentals and one-fourth of gross family income, less a $300 deduction for each dependent. As income rises, the tenant's payment increases and the rent supplement is reduced. Incomes are re-examined annually to determine the level of supplements and the tenant's contribution. If the family increases its earnings to the point where it can pay a market rent with one-fourth of income, no subsidy is given, but the family may, and is encouraged to, remain. Hopefully, a wider income range will be achieved as the incomes of some tenants rise.

Rent supplements are restricted to low-income families. Obviously, no supplements are given to families whose income exceeds four times the market rate on supplemented units; but, in addition, the family's initial income must be less than the maximum limits for public housing eligibility. Income can rise above this maximum and supplements may still be received, but to enter a rent-supplemented unit the family must be eligible for public housing. HUD has also set a minimum income requirement, with the administra-

tive regulation that rent supplements can amount to no mor
than 70 percent of market rents; or, in other words, that tenant
must be able to pay 30 percent of their rent. For instance, in a
efficiency apartment costing $125 monthly, the single occupan
would need an income of $1,800 annually or would have to pa
more than 25 percent of his income.

Rent supplements are not available to all families on the basi
of need. They are limited to occupants of specially designated
new or substantially rehabilitated housing. The supplement, whic
is paid directly to the landlord, is tied to the housing unit, an
eligible families can only receive supplements in such units. Un
like the leasing program, existing housing cannot be assisted un
less it is rehabilitated, and the explicit goal of the rent supplemen
program is to foster production of low-cost housing through it
long-term rental guarantees.

The way the program works is that the government signs con
tracts for up to forty years with nonprofit organizations, co-opera
tives, or limited-dividend corporations which sponsor new or re
habilitated housing projects. These contracts provide for continuin
supplements on a stated number of units within the propose
projects. The assurance of market rate rentals, and concomitan
FHA insurance, reduce the risk to outside lenders, making i
easier for the sponsor to find private financing. Once the projec
is completed, the investment can be amortized from the supple
mented rentals, while the tenants pay a reduced rent.

While the bulk of rent supplements are intended for project
financed at market interest rates (MIR) in the private market, 1
percent of the funds approved in appropriation acts are reserve
for special purposes—5 percent for use in BMIR projects and .
percent for use along with direct loans for housing for the elderly
The double subsidy achieved by combining rent supplements wit
these other forms of assistance allows them to reach lower-incom
families. But these special purpose supplements do not, by them
selves, increase the housing supply as do regular rent supplement
to MIR projects, and for this reason they have been limited b
legislation.

THE GOALS OF RENT SUPPLEMENTS

The rent supplement program was designed with three major aims in mind. First, and perhaps most important in terms of passage of the program, rent supplements were considered an alternative to low-interest direct loans. Direct loans require large initial resource commitments, and, from a budgetary perspective, they invert the relationship between payments and the housing services which are acquired. They are politically unattractive because they enter the budget as an expenditure in the year they are made. But the rent supplement approach, with its reliance on private financing, also has drawbacks. The contracts signed with private sponsors commit the government to long-term payments. New contracts for $50 million in annual rent supplements could mean as much as $2 billion in payments over forty years. But, far more crucially, the reliance on private financing ties the development of low-cost housing under rent supplements to the ups and downs of the private mortgage market. In times of general credit stringency, little can be done to attract private funds to low-cost housing. Increasing interest rates mean increasing project costs, larger supplements, and fewer families which can be helped with a fixed total subsidy authority.

Nonetheless, the chance to get away from direct loans and to have some immediate and measurable impact on the supply of low-cost housing was a strong selling point of the rent supplement program. President Johnson promoted it as a complete substitute for direct financing, claiming that "if it works as well as we expect, it should be possible to phase out most of our existing programs of low-interest loans."[1]

The second aim of the rent supplement program was to shift the ownership and operation of low-cost housing units to the private sector. It was hoped that private sector management would result in more efficient operation and that the social motivations of the nonprofit sponsors would provide more adequate service

---

[1] Morton J. Schussheim, *Toward A New Housing Policy* (New York: Committee for Economic Development, 1969), p. 15.

for the poor. With private ownership, taxes would be paid on rent-supplemented housing, rather than the 10 percent payment under public housing. This might triple the local revenue from the assisted project and would certainly increase its attractiveness at the local level.

The third aim of the rent supplement program was to disperse low-income families. It was intended that rent-supplemented tenants occupy only a minor portion of the units in any particular project, and that middle- and lower-income families would live side by side. With mixed projects, resistance in more affluent neighborhoods would hopefully diminish, and geographical dispersion could result as well. Low-income families might then take advantage of the superior social facilities in more affluent communities.

PRODUCTION OF RENT-SUPPLEMENTED UNITS

The performance of the rent supplement program has disappointed many. Through fiscal year 1969 only 16,567 supplemented units had been completed, and since many were in unfinished projects, only 12,299 were occupied at the year's end. These are broken down by type in Table 7.

The major cause of this limited performance was meager funding. Despite its rhetoric and the authorization of $150 million for the first four years, Congress appropriated only $72 million for rent supplement contracts through fiscal year 1969, and only $6.9 million was paid out in actual rent supplements on occupied units.

Table 7. Rent supplement completions through fiscal 1969

Type	Units occupied	Units ready
MIR	9,404	13,078
BMIR	688	860
Elderly	2,207	2,629
Total	12,299	16,567

SOURCE: Department of Housing and Urban Development.

56

able 8. **Rent supplement authorizations and payments** *(In millions)*

	Fiscal year 1966	Fiscal year 1967	Fiscal year 1968	Fiscal year 1969	Total
uthorized by legislation	$30	$35	$40	$45	$150
ontract authority granted	12	20	10	30	72
ayments made	—	.2	1.1	5.6	6.9

)URCE: Department of Housing and Urban Development.

In light of these very severe fiscal constraints, the quantitative :hievements of the rent supplement program are not as dis->pointing as its qualitative performance. Closer examination of ιe characteristics of the housing which has been subsidized and ιilt and of the families who occupy these units raises serious)ubts as to whether the rent supplement program has done what set out to do. It has achieved neither a wide range of incomes in 3 projects nor a dispersion of projects into more affluent com-.unities. Its success in luring private capital into low-income)using has been limited, and its projects have been difficult to itiate.

ιE FAILURE TO ACHIEVE AN INCOME MIX

The rent supplement program has come to serve an overwhelm-gly low-income and seriously disadvantaged clientele. A survey 4,307 families in market interest rate projects in January 1969 owed a median gross family income of only $2,400, less than e public housing median, for families averaging 3.3 members. ver 93 percent of these rent-supplemented families earned $4,000 less annually. For over half, assistance payments are the only urce of income, and they contribute to the income of another ι percent.

Given the characteristics of the rent supplement recipients, ere is very little likelihood that many will increase their income that rent supplements can be reduced and a mix of incomes can achieved. Certainly, the 63 percent of households living par-

57

tially or totally on assistance payments cannot expect any drastic increases in income. And though the disadvantaged workers may increase their earnings, it is doubtful that they will rise to a point where they can afford private housing of the rent-supplemented quality. Recertification data gathered so far supports this point. An internal survey of 268 of the earliest enrollees in the program showed that 37 percent had increased their earnings so that rent supplement payments could be reduced. This percentage is the same as the proportion with income from jobs alone, and these are in all likelihood the families who have increased their earnings. But for 68 percent of those sampled, rent supplements remained the same or increased.

If mixed incomes are unlikely to be achieved through the income gains of rent-supplemented families, they are even less likely to be achieved by the voluntary location of middle-income families in rent-supplemented projects. Because of cost limitations and limited amenities and because of the stigma of assisted housing, units in rent-supplemented projects are not attractive to more affluent families, and less than a third of the units in projects with rent supplement contracts are unsupplemented. And even this overstates the income mix. Table 9 breaks out the proportion of supplemented units by type of project. Clearly, when the rent supplement is used alone, rather than in conjunction with other forms of assistance, the projects which are built are completely rent-supplemented. The apparent mix of supplemented and unsupplemented families is only the cohabilitation of low-income

Table 9. Type of projects and sponsors as of April 11, 1969

Type of project	Total units	Supplemented units	Percent supplemented
MIR	53,540	53,495	99.9
202, 221d3	31,807	7,390	23.2
236	1,461	289	19.8
State-assisted	371	75	20.2
Total	87,179	61,249	70.2

SOURCE: Department of Housing and Urban Development.

families receiving subsidies through other assistance programs and the even lower-income families receiving rent supplements in addition. As envisioned in the original design of the rent supplement program—families of significantly different incomes, standards, and values living side by side—there is no income mix.

THE LOCATION OF RENT-SUPPLEMENTED UNITS

The geographic dispersion of rent supplement projects has been only slightly more successful than the attempt to mix income groups in the same project. Of the total unit reservations as of September 30, 1969, 31 percent were in blighted areas, another 36 percent in the core city, and only 9 percent were in the suburbs. Core cities are not uniformly distressed areas, but they are hardly the more affluent neighborhoods envisioned as potential locations. Less than one-third of all rent-supplemented units are dispersed into more stable neighborhoods in the suburbs or within the city limits outside of blighted or core areas.

The major reason is that because of their uniformly low-income tenantry, rent supplement projects are little more acceptable to affluent communities than public housing. But another reason is clearly the Spartan cost limitations which HUD has administratively imposed. In the 1966 appropriations hearings, HUD Secretary Robert C. Weaver gave exact and stringent specifications, assuring Congress, under pressure, that there would be no "frills" in rent-supplemented units, such as air conditioners or more than one toilet (even in a four-bedroom apartment). HUD has been equally strict in setting dollar cost limits, and despite increases recently to allow for increases in interest costs, the limits are so low that in most large cities even minimal quality units cannot be constructed. A 25 percent mark-up is allowed in high-cost areas, but this has not proved adequate.

These cost limits have skewed the distribution of rent supplement projects, leading to a preponderance of new construction in the South and Southwest. The San Francisco and New York regions together have less than half the combined reservations of the

59

Atlanta and Fort Worth regions. As of September 30, 1969, cities with a population over 100,000 had 42,000 unit reservations compared with 38,000 for smaller cities, but few of these were in the largest cities, unless they were rehabilitation projects. Of the little over 6,000 rehabilitations, five-sixths were in cities over 100,000, where cost limits would generally not permit new construction.

OBSTACLES TO THE DEVELOPMENT OF RENT SUPPLEMENT HOUSING

There has also been some apparent difficulty in developing new units with the rent supplement guarantee alone. According to HUD estimates, 70 percent of occupied units in fiscal year 1968 and 30 percent in fiscal year 1969 were in BMIR or housing projects for the elderly. At the end of fiscal year 1969, 24 percent of occupied units and 21 percent of completed units were located in these other projects. The reason is clearly that MIR projects have taken longer and been more difficult to develop, while BMIR and housing for the elderly were already being completed at the beginning of the program. The first new MIR project was not even announced until February 1967 because of the 1966 credit crunch which cut off almost all private funds for mortgages; and in the first two years of rent supplements, almost all went to 202 projects. But HUD claims to have used less than 10 percent of its approved contract authority for units in BMIR and housing projects for the elderly. Though 13.5 percent of reserved units were in such projects at the end of fiscal 1969, the average contracted payments were less because of the piggyback on other subsidies, and legislative stipulations were met.

Nonetheless, new construction has felt the pinch of tight money and it has also been hindered by the limitations of its nonprofit and limited-dividend sponsors, as contrasted with the eager and competent efforts of private developers in many areas under leasing and turnkey. Red tape has also been a significant problem. In trying to insure against profit-seekers, HUD developed com-

plicated application procedures; Urban America's handbook for
rent supplement sponsors came to 323 pages. The result was that
processing times averaged eighteen months in the program's first
four years. New methods were introduced in the summer of 1969
and are expected to cut processing time to less than six months;
but up to the present, red tape has been a serious obstacle, especially relative to the much simpler turnkey methods of public
housing.

THE ASSETS OF RENT SUPPLEMENTS

When the rent supplement program was introduced in 1965,
President Johnson described it as "the most crucial new instrument in our effort to improve the American city."[2] Clearly, it has
fallen short of these expectations. With limited funding and a
concentration on new construction, unit completions have been
few. The program has had little success in achieving a range of
incomes in its projects or in dispersing them throughout the community; it has been directed to an extremely low-income clientele,
which has discouraged middle-income families from living in rent
supplement projects and has made them unattractive to more
affluent neighborhoods. Despite these shortcomings the rent supplement program has developed into a useful assistance tool.
While it is by no means a "crucial instrument," it has an important role to play.

For one thing, rent supplements reach a lower-income clientele
than any other program except public housing. These families
are not being adequately served elsewhere, and even public housing has its problems in reaching down to these levels though recent
changes promise to improve the situation. Rent supplements are
especially effective when used as a double subsidy, to integrate extremely low-income families into projects developed with other forms
of assistance. Most of the income mix which has been achieved by
the rent supplement program has come in this way, placing the

[2] *Ibid.*, p. 15.

lowest-income families among the higher but still low-income tenants of other assisted projects. However, only 10 percent of the aggregate rent supplement authorizations may be used in this manner, and it might be wise to increase the proportion used as double subsidy.

The major purpose of the rent supplement program is to develop new housing, using private rather than public funds and sponsors. In this use, it is similar to the leased housing program when newly constructed units are leased. The two tools have many similarities, and comparisons are inevitable because the programs were launched at the same time, with highly partisan support.

Superficially, the leased housing program has been far more successful than rent supplements. At the end of fiscal 1969, 12,300 supplemented units were occupied, compared with 54,304 leased units at the end of 1969. But the larger figures under the leasing program must be discounted by the fact that 69 percent were already existing without rehabilitation and only 7 percent or 3,800, were comparable with the new units being built under the rent supplement program. Rent supplement occupancies have been limited, chiefly because the program has focused on new construction, with its consequent lags in output.

The rent supplement may, in fact, be the better tool to stimulate new construction. Its sponsors are either nonprofit or limited-dividend groups, rather than unlimited profit-seekers, and they are likely to show more concern for the needs of their projected clientele. The rent supplement contracts run for a much longer period, giving more assurance to the developer than a short-term lease and also providing a longer-run guarantee of housing for low-income families. Before development is initiated the rent supplement guarantee is signed openly and with no question of payment, offering the public perhaps a greater degree of control over costs than under leasing. And, finally, the rent supplement program was designed for this purpose and does not have to be distorted to be used for new construction like the leasing program.

6

The 236 Rental Housing Program

The public housing, leasing, and rent supplement programs focus on the housing needs of the lowest-income families and individuals. But there are many households who are not poor and yet are still unable to afford adequate housing. Several programs have been developed to assist such families, and a different subsidy technique has been used—the below-market interest rate (BMIR). Through a direct loan or an interest subsidy on a private loan, the interest rate is reduced, lowering interest payments on development costs and facilitating lower rents. The subsidy under this technique varies with the market and subsidized rates, but its maximum is the total interest cost. This may not be adequate to meet the needs of the lowest-income families; however, for those who can make some meaningful contribution to their housing costs, it provides the needed assistance.

The BMIR technique was first used in 1961 under the 221 (d) (3) program, which provided special assistance funds to the Federal National Mortgage Association for the purchase of low-income project mortgages bearing a reduced interest rate. Originally set at the cost of federal borrowing, the BMIR was fixed at 3 percent in 1965. Under 221(d)(3), 142,000 units were financed through fiscal 1969, although only a little over half were in completed projects at the end of the year.

The BMIR was also used in the 202 elderly housing program, which provided fifty-year, 3 percent loans to nonprofit sponsors of housing designed for elderly occupants. These loans were made directly from a revolving fund with its own authorizations and appropriations. Operating since 1959, the 202 program had financed 45,527 units as of September 1969, and 27,780 of these had been completed.

Both of these BMIR programs were only beginning to fulfill expectations in 1968 when they were replaced by the 236 rental housing program. Future loans were curtailed and projects in the pipeline were transferred where possible to the 236 program. The major reason for this change was that both 202 and 221(d) (3) relied on government financing. The opposition to using public credit for housing was not allayed by the rent supplement program, which had been modified during passage to serve a lower-income group and was not a substitute for 202 and 221(d)(3). For this reason, a new tool was devised—the interest subsidy. Though 236 is also a BMIR program, the reduced rates are achieved through interest subsidy payments to private mortgagors, rather than through direct government loans; private credit is meant to be used rather than public sources.

This new 236 program has a variety of goals. Like the rent supplement program, it seeks to mix families of different incomes in its projects, to disperse these projects into more affluent neighborhoods, and primarily to tap private credit sources rather than use government funds. Like the 202 and 221(d)(3) programs, it focuses on those with incomes above public housing levels, who can make substantial contributions to their housing costs but are still unable to afford adequate housing. It is also meant to breach the gap which developed between the rent supplement–public housing clientele and that of the 202 and 221(d)(3) programs. Under both the earlier BMIR programs, rents were calculated to cover expenses and amortization of the 3 percent rate, and there was no provision for rents to be based on occupants' income; project sponsors tended to charge all families a rent which would cover the basic payment at the 3 percent rate and to select only those households which could afford it. For instance, in the 202 program, half of the assisted households consisted of single persons and most of the remainder were two-member families, yet less than 30 percent had an income of under $2,000 and less than 16 percent of under $1,500, which are, roughly speaking, the poverty levels for two-person and single-person elderly households. Similar crowding at the upper income limits was experienced in 221(d)(3)–BMIR projects, and there was a gap between families covered by public housing and rent supplements and those assisted by 202 and 221(d)(3)–BMIR. This was to be breached by the 236 program.

THE DESIGN OF 236

Under 236, periodic payments are made to private lenders who have financed low-income rental and co-operative housing projects. These payments amount to the difference between monthly debt expenses at market interest rates and those which would prevail at a 1 percent rate.

The project sponsor and mortgagee is the immediate beneficiary, since his debt payments are reduced. To guarantee that these reductions are passed on to occupants as lower rents, restrictions are placed on eligible sponsors. They must be either nonprofit groups, co-operatives, or limited-dividend corporations. Nonprofits and co-operatives present no particular problem and are easily policed to insure against abuse. But the limited-dividend corporations are more carefully regulated. They are required to put up 10 percent of the development cost, and they are then limited to a 6 percent return on this investment. Additional payments are provided for construction or management services, amounting to from 4 to 6 percent of construction costs and 3 percent of gross rent rolls, respectively. Though these profits are not very large, they are certain. Extended tax shelter is also provided, with recent changes in the tax law permitting the investor to get extraordinarily attractive depreciation treatment through the use of double declining balance on the total development costs of new 236 properties. The result is that 236 investments are fairly attractive to individuals and groups forming limited-dividend corporations, and these have sponsored most 236 projects.

Out of the rent collected each month, the sponsor retains a *basic payment* which covers all operating and management costs, debt retirement expenses, and profits in the case of limited-dividend corporations. Debt expenses are, of course, reduced by the interest subsidy, since the sponsor pays 1 percent on his mortgage instead of a market rate, and the profits are either limited or nonexistent.

The rent charged to the occupants of 236 projects is based on their income. The household pays one-fourth of its adjusted income, less $300 deductions for each minor. A family of four with $4,200 income annually would thus pay a monthly rent of $75. As the family income increases, its rent also increases until it is paying a market rate.

Out of this monthly rental, the project sponsor retains the basic payment and any excess is returned to the government and placed in a revolving fund. As family income and rent increase, more is returned to the government and the subsidy decreases. If market rents can be paid from one-fourth of income and the family continues to live in the project as it is encouraged to do, the whole interest subsidy amount is returned monthly; while, if the family can afford only the basic payment, none is returned and the maximum interest subsidy is being received.

The interest subsidy under 236 works like this. On a $15,000 rental unit, $115 would be paid in monthly principal and interest expenses on a thirty-year mortgage at the current FHA "market" rate of 8 ½ percent. At a 1 percent rate, debt expenses would be only $48 monthly, and this is the amount paid by the borrower, with the difference of $67 contributed by the government. If a family of four with $4,200 income lived in this unit and paid a

$75 monthly rent, the sponsor would retain $48 plus whatever was needed for maintenance and operation and would return the rest to the government.

At a minimum, the household must meet the basic payment. If this were not paid by all occupants, the project would be operating at a deficit and the sponsor would lack the funds needed for operation, profit, and debt retirement. But this basic payment may be subsidized from some other source, reducing the minimum necessary income. For instance, rent supplements can be used in 236 projects to make up the difference between the basic payment and what the family can pay with a fourth of its income, and 25 percent of all projects under reservation as of December 31, 1969, were rent-supplemented. However, there is a 40 percent legislative limit and a 20 percent administrative limit on the proportion of rent-supplemented units in any particular project to insure that individual projects do not become dominated by a single low-income class. Though a fourth of 236 projects have rent-supplemented units, probably less than 5 percent of all units are rent-supplemented.

There are other income restrictions under 236. To be eligible for occupancy in assisted projects, the household must ordinarily have an adjusted income which is less than 135 percent of the maximum public housing income limits. However, 20 percent of authorized funds may be used for households whose incomes are initially higher than these limits, but less than 90 percent of the income limits for occupancy in 221(d)(3)–BMIR rental housing. The second and higher limit provides for areas where construction costs are high relative to public housing maximums, and where basic payments on 236 projects cannot be met with a fourth of these maximums. Public housing and 221(d)(3) limits vary from county to county, and it is difficult to generalize on how they interact with local construction costs. The regular 236 entrance limits range from $4,000 to more than $9,000 for a family of four, with most between $5,000 and $7,000; the 90 percent of 221(d)(3) limits are usually several hundred dollars higher.

Unlike the rent supplement program, there are no specific cost limits under 236. The mortgage on any one project cannot exceed $12.5 million, but this limits the number of units and not their average cost. Implicitly, however, the maximum income limits put an over-all ceiling on what occupants can pay and thus on costs, and the projects must be designed so that basic payments will be less than one-fourth of these maximums. This is not as much of a constraint as it might be, since in high-cost areas the 90 percent of 221(d)(3) limits can be used if funds for this purpose are available.

LOCATION OF 236 UNITS

The 236 program was initiated to replace and improve upon the earlier 202 and 221(d)(3)–BMIR programs. It is difficult to judge its success because, as of June 30, 1969, only eight projects had been started and these will not be occupied until early in 1970. But some conclusions can be drawn from reservations for units to be built as soon as possible.

The program seems to have done fairly well in dispersing projects outside of blighted areas and core cities. Since it is intended to serve a lower-income clientele on the average than either 202 or 221(d)(3)–BMIR, greater difficulty might be expected in penetrating more stable neighborhoods. This apparently has not been the case. At the end of 1969 there were 572 projects under preliminary reservation and 139 under firm obligation, altogether accounting for an estimated 90,000 units. Table 10 compares the distribution of these units with those under the 202, 221(d)(3)–BMIR and rent supplement programs. No 202 projects are supposedly located in blighted areas; this is agency policy and it is not too difficult to achieve since communities are rarely opposed to housing for the elderly. And, likewise, none of the housing strictly for the elderly under 236—2 percent of its reservations—is located in blighted areas. Relative to both 221(d) (3)–BMIR and rent supplements, the 236 program is obviously doing better in reaching suburban areas and locations within the cities but outside their blighted and core areas.

Table 10. Locational characteristics of unit reservations under various assistance programs, September 30, 1969

	Blighted area	Core city	City limits	Suburbs
221(d)(3)–BMIR				
projects	36%	15%	33%	13%
202 units	0	58	34	8
Rent supplement units	29	35	26	10
236 units	32	5	48	15

SOURCE: Department of Housing and Urban Development.

The regional distribution of 236 reservations has not been a problem as it was under the rent supplement and 221(d)(3)– BMIR programs, since there are no explicit cost limits. Almost all regions seem to be actively and equally participating in 236. One fact which is difficult to explain is the smaller number of 236 reservations in the largest cities relative to the other BMIR programs. The ten largest cities had received 22 percent of 221(d) (3)–BMIR final endorsements as of June 30, 1969, but only 12 percent of 236 reservations at the end of the year.

THE CONSEQUENCES OF PRIVATE FUNDING UNDER 236

The major difference between 236 and the earlier 221(d)(3)– BMIR and 202 programs is its reliance on private credit. The 202 loans came from a revolving fund with separate authorizations, and 221(d)(3)–BMIR mortgages were purchased from the FNMA and later GNMA special assistance funds augmented specifically for this purpose. The 236 mortgages, on the other hand, were intended for private lenders who would receive interest subsidies from the government. But tight money has dried up the sources of private financing, so that the government has had to step in. The Government National Mortgage Association has been authorized to purchase up to $650 million in 236 mortgages at a discount, and then to sell them at par to its "private" sister, the FNMA, under a technique called the "tandem plan." In more normal conditions, however, 236 mortgages are to be purchased by regular mortgage institutions, such as savings and

69

loans, banks, and insurance companies. This could have several possible effects.

One is that the sponsor's role under the 236 program may be reduced, especially relative to the 202 program. Instead of dealing with the government, which is lenient in its debt management and permits nonprofit groups a major degree of control over project specifications and development, these groups must now deal with private financial institutions which are stricter and demand a degree of control themselves. These financial institutions have little concern with project cost, since the return on their loan is guaranteed. The 236 projects are built on a cost-plus-fixed-fee basis rather than through competitive bids as in 202. And there are additional costs involved in introducing a third party into these transactions. The end result is that 236 will probably cost more than 202 housing. This has been the case to date. Nearly one-tenth of 236 reservations as of December 31, 1969, were conversions from 202 projects, and the consistent experience has been that changing from one basis to another increases development costs an average of nearly $1,500 a unit.

These project cost increases are more a problem relative to 202 than to the 221(d)(3). While nonprofits, especially churches, have long played an active role in housing for the elderly and seem willing and able to make substantial contributions of time and money, their interest in nonelderly low-income housing is much more limited. Despite a few notable successes, the experience with nonprofits under 221(d)(3) has generally been unfavorable; they were often understaffed, lacking technical expertise and the resources to meet continuing financial responsibilities. An analysis of 221(d)(3) projects in Philadelphia found that "FHA officials expressed candid cynicism towards the involvement of nonprofit sponsors. They obviously prefer to deal with experienced, profit-motivated firms in producing such housing."[1]

Thus, there is probably little loss and some gain in giving more

[1] Henry Toland, "Non-Profit Housing Lags In City, Gaining In Suburbs," *Philadelphia Bulletin*, January 26, 1970, p. 5.

control to financial institutions under 236 relative to 221(d)(3)–BMIR. They are more likely to weed out less-qualified project sponsors and they will demand fiscally sound operations. But for housing for the elderly the nonprofits are better qualified and there is a very definite loss in using the 236 rather than the 202 approach. Congress reacted to the displeasure of nonprofit elderly-housing groups when it increased the authorizations for 202 by $150 million in the Housing and Urban Development Act of 1969. However, the Administration and HUD are not seeking any appropriations, still intending to phase 202 into 236 to avoid direct loans. It may be wise for Congress to follow through on the authorization with specific appropriations if it feels that emphasis is still needed on privately owned housing for the elderly.

These initial cost considerations are important, but the long-run differences between the interest subsidy and direct financing techniques are far more significant. Over time, interest subsidies cost substantially more than direct loans. The current long-term federal borrowing rate is around 6 ½ percent, while the FHA rate on new 236 project mortgages is 8 ½ percent. The government thus pays an extra 2 percent on the outstanding mortgage amount in order to use private funds. On every $15,000, thirty-year mortgage, this means that the government pays $20 more monthly, or $7,200 over the life of the mortgage, increasing subsidy costs by one-third. This over-simplifies the difference, but it gives an idea of the very substantial costs involved in substituting interest subsidies for direct loans.

The only rationale for these higher costs is budgetary. Under a direct loan program the full amount of the loan would be an entry, even though it represents a capital expenditure, while under 236, only the annual contracted interest subsidies enter the budget. Through the interest subsidy approach, more housing is supplied for any given appropriation than through direct loans. But over time the aggregate appropriations for a given number of interest-subsidized units are substantially more than those needed for an equal number provided through direct loans. The government unquestionably gets more for its dollar through direct loans. However, if appropriations continue to be limited, and if Congress remains unwilling to make the immediate and large-scale commitment of resources needed for a direct loan program, then the higher price of subsidizing private loans must be paid if a significant number of units is to be built.

OPERATION BREAKTHROUGH

A sizable portion of 236 funds, and of those allocated to the 235 program discussed in the next chapter, have been reserved for a special purpose; approximately $15 million from the two programs will be used for research and development grants to private firms, assisting them to produce lower-cost, technologically advanced housing. It is hoped that localities will help by updating building codes, and unions by changing restrictive work practices, so that substantial economies can result through the wider use of industrialized production methods. The effort has been titled "Operation Breakthrough," with the implication that substantial cost reductions can be achieved.

Operation Breakthrough is based on the legislative mandate of Section 108 of the Housing and Urban Development Act of 1968, which directed HUD's Secretary to use existing program funds for large-scale experiments with industrialized housing. Up to five plans were to be approved with up to 1,000 units annually to be constructed under each plan over a five-year period. This would total 25,000 units over the five years, providing an adequate test of mass production techniques. The leverage of guaranteed employment could be used to negotiate concessions by unions at the local level, and the location of these units could be predicated on the modernization of local building codes.

Unfortunately, Operation Breakthrough has a much smaller scale. It contemplates around 3,000 units produced by some twenty private firms and located in "housing fairs" in ten cities. Though some of the corporate giants are among the developers initially selected, including Republic and U.S. Steel, Dow Chemical, Martin-Marietta, Alcoa, Westinghouse, and General Electric, each will produce only 100 to 150 units, which is hardly mass production. Their initial proposals do not suggest any technological breakthroughs. Sites have already been selected, without changes in building codes, and unions will undoubtedly comply as an exception. In other words, the best that can happen is that a few large firms will get involved in housing for the first time, and a few demonstration units will be built, testing new methods and increasing consumer acceptance. Mass production economies will not be realized.

There are a number of firms who could presently mass produce housing at a lower cost, using well-tested methods. What they need is a guaranteed market; one which would insure the sale of at least 1,000 units a year for five years as envisioned in Section 108. This could be provided under 236 and 235 by requiring a regional and local co-ordination of purchases, and since these programs are already being used in Operation Breakthrough, it would seem natural to further co-ordinate their commitments and also to use other programs to purchase from mass-producers of Breakthrough housing.

7

The 235 Homeownership Plan

GOALS OF 235

The oft-repeated goal of a "decent home and suitable living environment for every American family" has usually been interpreted in the strictly material sense—"four walls, a roof that doesn't leak, and indoor plumbing for every low-income household." Given the vast numbers of physically ill-housed, there has been little attention to the other aspects of housing, such as the amenities which it offers, the life-style it promotes, or the security it provides. For the majority of American families, these other aspects are best realized through homeownership, and the major focus of federal housing policy outside of the subsidy programs has been support for homebuyers through mortgage insurance and special tax treatment. But lower-income families cannot take advantage of these programs. They need more direct forms of assistance if they are to realize the benefits of homeownership, and until recently these have not been provided.

In the Housing and Urban Development Act of 1968, Congress initiated the first major program of direct subsidies for homeownership—the 235 program. It was intended for families in the $3,000 to $8,000 income range—those who cannot afford homeownership without financial assistance, but who have a dependable income and can make a substantial contribution. By subsidizing their demand, 235 hoped to stimulate construction and rehabilitation activity. Its goal was to increase the low-cost housing stock rather than to merely transfer ownership of existing units to lower-income families. And, in fact, specific limits were originally set on the portions of contract authority which could be used for existing housing: not more than 25 percent through fiscal 1969; 15 percent in fiscal 1970; and 10 percent in fiscal 1971. After that, all assisted units were to be new, except in the cases where they could not be provided economically. It was hoped that these new units could be dispersed into more stable communities. Since single-family units were being developed, rather than rental projects with their concentrated low-income populations, more success was anticipated under 235 than under 236.

PROGRAM DESIGN

Under 235 the eligible homebuyer is supposed to finance his purchase with a private, FHA-insured mortgage. Only minimal downpayments are required, amounting to $200 for most families or 3 percent for those whose income is more than 135 percent of public housing admission maximums. The government then contributes to monthly mortgage payments, making up the difference between one-fifth of the family's income (less a $25 monthly deduction for each child) and monthly payments for principal, interest, taxes, and home and mortgage insurance. The maximum government contribution is the difference between monthly payments on the FHA-insured mortgage, which has a current maximum of 8.5 percent and ½ percent insurance premium, and the monthly payments which would be required on a mortgage with a 1 percent interest rate. For instance, on a thirty-year, $15,000 mortgage at 8.5 percent, the estimated monthly payments would be $155, including principal and interest payments of $115, $30 to taxes, a mortgage insurance premium of $6, and $4 for home insurance. At a 1 percent rate, debt expenses for principal and interest would be only $48, so that the maximum federal contribution would be the difference between this and the $121 which would otherwise be paid for principal, interest, and mortgage insurance. The subsidy would amount to $73 of the $155 on monthly mortgage-related payments.

The proportion of income paid by the homebuyer is 20 percent under the 235 program, as compared with 25 percent under the 236 and rent supplement programs. This lower proportion is based on the assumption that the maintenance and operating costs paid by the homeowner in addition to his mortgage payments will make up this difference. In the 235 program, as in 236, the amount of assistance is reduced if the family's income rises. The family, of course, continues the mortgage payments without subsidy if income rises so that it can do this with less than one-fifth of its income. There is a recertification of income every two years.

To occupy 235 housing, the family should be able, at a minimum, to meet the monthly principal and interest payments on a 1 percent mortgage; or, in other words, its income should be five times this amount. From the example, if the subsidy is $73, leaving $82 to be paid by the homeowner with one-fifth of his income, an annual income of $4,920 is required, excluding deductions. Lower-income families must buy lower-cost homes if they are to spend only a reasonable share of their income, but there are minimum costs to even low-quality homes. Only 2 percent of all 235 homes have been purchased for less than $8,000, which would require an estimated $2,750 in income, excluding deductions. This necessarily limits the lower income of families who can reasonably participate in 235.

There are also limits on the maximum income of families subsidized under 235. Obviously, if it rises to the point where the family can pay full debt costs with one-fifth of its income, no further subsidy will be received. In the example, the maximum subsidized income would be five times the mortgage-related expenses of $155, or $9,300 annually. On a larger mortgage, payments and allowable income would be higher. However, there are statutory limits to the size of 235 home mortgages. For smaller families, they cannot exceed $18,000, except in high-cost areas where the limit is $21,000. For families with five or more members, the limits are increased to $21,000 and $24,000, respectively.

There are explicit income limits for initial occupancy in addition to the implicit limits on the incomes which can be subsidized. To be initially eligible, the family must usually earn less than 135 percent of the maximum income limits for public housing. As in the 236 program, 20 percent of 235 funds are reserved for families earning more than this amount, but less than 90 percent of the 221(d)(3) eligibility maximums. Since these are locally established, 235 eligibility limits vary from place to place and, of course, are dependent on the size of the family. As a general example, 135 percent of the public housing maximum in Boston for a family of three is $7,320, and 90 percent of the 221(d)(3) maximum is slightly higher, $7,830. These are probably typical, with the normal maximum for a family of four being roughly $8,000, although lower in the South and Southwest.

THE SUCCESS OF 235

On the whole, 235 has been popular, and effective in housing a large number of families in short order, though its long-run impact and its success in making homeowners of low-income families cannot be known. Through October 1969, 15,983 units were occupied under the program, which is more than the rent supplement program had achieved in four years of operation.

These 235 units are clearly serving the clientele for which they were intended—stable families in the $3,000 to $8,000 income range. A HUD survey of 235 transactions insured in the third quarter of fiscal 1969 found that the typical family, consisting of five persons, had a gross annual income of $5,685. Few families were in severe poverty, with only 2 percent having incomes of less than $3,000; and few had more than a moderate income, with only 7 percent earning more than $8,000 annually.

After deductions for dependents, the median certified income was $4,464. Without the 235 subsidy few of these families could have purchased their homes, which had an average cost of $15,000.

The program has been fairly successful in dispersing these families outside blighted and core city areas, much more so than any other subsidy program. As of June 16, 1969, only 10 percent of its 20,000 reservations were inside blighted areas, and 5 percent in core cities: some 61 percent were within city limits but outside the core, and 24 percent were located in the suburbs. In other words, 85 percent of 235 units were in more attractive neighborhoods, compared with 53 and 36 percent, respectively, under the 236 and rent supplement programs. Unfortunately, there is no data on the racial mix in 235 housing, and the impression is that its success is due in large part to "creaming" of the clientele it serves, for instance, by the choice of "low-income" families whose head is in college.

HOMEOWNERSHIP COSTS IN EXCESS OF ONE-FIFTH OF INCOME

The 235 program has been successful despite several shortcomings in its design. For one thing, families must often pay an exorbitant share of their income for homeownership, even with subsidies. Though 235 recipients pay only 20 percent of their income, as compared with 25 percent under 236, the related expenses of homeownership frequently require more than 5 percent of the homeowner's income, making housing costs substantially greater. As an example, Table 11 breaks down the typical housing costs in the Boston Model Cities Area. Of the total housing costs of $180, $52 are operating expenses and must be paid by the owner in addition to his 20 percent contribution. This will raise his total housing costs to more than one-quarter of his income. For instance, with a $4,800 annual income after deductions, the family will pay 20 percent of its income, or $80 monthly, toward the $128 mortgage-related costs. It must then pay maintenance and operating expenses of $52 for a total monthly housing cost of $132. This is one-third rather than one-fourth of

Table 11.   Monthly housing costs in the Boston model cities area

Housing costs subject to subsidy		$128
Mortgage premium and interest	$96	
Mortgage insurance	4	
Taxes	20	
Fire and hazard insurance	8	
Unsubsidized owner's expense		52
Heat	17	
Gas and electric	6	
Maintenance and reserve	25	
Sewer and water	4	
Total housing costs		$180

SOURCE: Frank S. and Mary C. Sengstock, "Homeownership: A Goal For All Americans," *Journal of Urban Law*, vol. 46, issue 3.

monthly income. If the family's income after deductions were only $3,000, it would have to pay almost half; and even if it were $7,200, nearly 30 percent would be needed if costs were as shown.

Because the family is responsible for maintenance and operating expenses beyond its 20 percent contribution, ownership under 235 is more costly than rental under 236. More seriously, a family with a lower income must pay a larger proportion of its income for a house of a given price. Another effect is that the 235 program is more attractive in low-cost areas with amenable climate. Maintenance and operating expenses may be less than half as much in some Southern and Southwestern areas as they are in the Northeast. If monthly costs were $22 rather than the $52 average in Boston, a family with $4,800 income in one of these low-cost areas would pay only one-fourth rather than one-third of its income for housing. The cost limits on 235 mortgages also work against high-cost areas, and the end result is a highly skewed geographical distribution. The Southern and Southwestern regions received 46 percent of reservations and obligations as of June 30, 1969, while the Northeast and Mid-Atlantic regions together received less than 15 percent.

THE PRODUCTION OF NEW HOUSING UNDER 235

The primary purpose of 235 is to stimulate the construction of new housing, and it was originally intended that by now, existing units would account for only a very small proportion of current reservations. Though the proportion of new housing has been increasing, little more than half of 235 reservations were being made for new construction at the end of fiscal 1969; and 9,089 of the 15,983 completed and occupied units through October 1969 were existing units. An estimated 4 ½ percent of these are substantially rehabilitated, but the remainder are "as is" purchases. Recognizing HUD's difficulty in reaching the stipulated ratios, which would have required that only 15 percent of funds be used for existing units in fiscal 1970, the 1969 Housing and Urban Development Act increased the ratio to 30 percent of all authority in fiscal 1970 and 1971 which may be used to subsidize the purchase of existing homes. The FHA, however, has announced that no funds will be available in 1970 for such purposes and that only new and substantially rehabilitated units will be accepted.

But experience to date with 235 raises doubt whether the guarantee of a government-supported market for low-cost, single-family housing alone will lead to a substantial increase in supply. There is already a large and unsubsidized market for this cheaper housing, as witnessed by the phenomenal success of the few large companies mass-producing cheaper housing and by the equally phenomenal growth of the mobile home industry. Without technological or organizational changes within the industry it is doubtful that lower-cost housing of more conventional types can be provided to meet the demand. At present, single-family units cannot be built in many large cities within the 235 maximum, and it is especially difficult to build for larger families. Of the units insured under the 235 program in the third quarter of 1969, only 24 percent of the new ones were for families of six or more members, compared with 42 percent of the existing units. If strict cost limits are maintained, the 235 program must continue to finance a substantial number of existing home purchases for these larger families, who probably benefit most from homeownership. These problems make the cost savings of Operation Breakthrough all the more important; these are needed as much and perhaps more for single-family, owner-occupied units than for multi-family rental dwellings.

THE EFFECTS OF THE INTEREST SUBSIDY TECHNIQUE

One of the greatest drawbacks of 235 is inherent in its interest subsidy technique. Mortgages come from "private" sources at market (FHA) rates, and payment terms are based on these rates. The federal contribution helps the low-income family to meet these terms, and reduces the interest rate it pays. But this is not the same thing to the homebuyer as a direct loan at the lower rate. The difference is that the equity build-up on an interest-subsidized loan is much smaller than on a direct low-interest rate loan. For instance, after fifteen years of payment on a thirty-year, $15,000 loan at the 8.5 percent FHA rate, the homebuyer will have accumulated only $3,200 in equity. If, instead, the government had provided a direct loan to the homebuyer at a 1 percent rate, he would have $6,950 in equity after fifteen years. Under either approach, he would make the same contribution based on his income, but, obviously, the direct loan would yield him more benefits. For the low-income family, homeownership is, more than anything else, a source of financial security. As a study of homeownership motivations concluded:

> Equity represents the investment-security factor of homeownership. It is especially important to low-income persons, for whom homeownership is the only practical means for establishing a savings program and securing thereby some degree of financial independence. For them, homeownership is a form of security against financial adversity in the future.[1]

[1] Frank S. and Mary C. Sengstock, "Homeownership: A Goal For All Americans," *Journal of Urban Law*, vol. 46, issue 3, University of Detroit, p. 375.

This suggests that the interest subsidy technique is not very well suited to a homeownership program, since it detracts from one of homeownership's most important benefits—the financial security it provides. Since a direct loan at reduced rates is cheaper in terms of federal expenditures over the long-run, it would appear to be a better alternative. This is especially the case since the GNMA and FNMA are so actively involved in the financing of 235 and will become even more so with the issuance of mortgage-backed securities by GNMA. So far, $500 million has been provided through the tandem purchase of 235 mortgages which is little different from a direct loan. There is no reason to maintain the fiction of an interest subsidy when for the same costs a lower-interest rate could be written into the terms of 235 mortgages.

8

Rehabilitation Programs

SCOPE OF REHABILITATION

Federal housing policy has always emphasized new construction, but in recent years rehabilitation has gained more attention, with an increase in its share of subsidized production. The estimated total of completed rehabilitations under HUD's programs at the end of fiscal 1969 was less than 40,000 units. But in 1968 some 24,300 rehabilitations were begun, which amounted to almost one-fifth of new construction starts. In 1969 rehabilitations expanded to 34,600 units or almost one-fourth of new construction starts.

There are a large number of rehabilitation tools. All the subsidy programs discussed so far provide for rehabilitation, though it usually accounts for only a small proportion of their activity. There are also two which are solely for rehabilitation, the 312 loan program and the 115 grant program. The rural loan programs administered by the Department of Agriculture also have large rehabilitation components, accounting for 27 percent of their starts in 1968 and 25 percent in 1969, but these will be discussed separately in the following chapter on rural programs.

The role of these various tools in the aggregate rehabilitation effort is indicated in Table 12.

Table 12. Rehabilitation activity under HUD's assistance programs

Program	Cumulative completed units as of April 29, 1969	Percent of completed units	Rehabilitation starts 1969	Percent of starts
312 loans	11,300	30%	11,800	34%
115 grants	7,000	18		
Public housing				
Turnkey	3,767	10	700	2
Acquisition	7,774	21	5,900	17
Leased housing	2,700	7	9,600	28
Rent supplement	891	2	700	2
221(d)(3)–BMIR	3,655	10	3,500	10
221h	448	1	1,700	5
235	—	—	400	1
236	—	—	300	1
Total	37,535	100%	34,600	100%

Source: Department of Housing and Urban Development.

312 Loans and 115 Grants

The two major rehabilitation tools are the 312 direct loan program and the 115 grant program. Under 312, low-interest loans are provided to owners and tenants of property in urban renewal and code enforcement areas. These are for rehabilitation and not for acquisition and are made only to property owners. They are fairly flexible. Nonresidential as well as residential rehabilitations can be financed, and investor-owners as well as resident-owners may receive them. However, four-fifths of all loans go to owner-occupants for residential rehabilitations.

These 312 loans are for a maximum of $10,000, with up to 45 percent extra in high-cost areas; they carry a BMIR of 3 percent and are available for up to twenty years or three-fourths of the remaining life of the rehabilitated property, whichever is less. A loan for the rehabilitation of residential property may also include an amount to refinance existing debt on the property, if the total debt payments exceed one-fifth of the owner's income. Owners of more than four-unit properties are not eligible for this refinancing

86

which is one reason for the small proportion of 312 loans going to investor-owners, who are not sufficiently attracted by the BMIR on loans which cover only the cost of rehabilitation.

Under the Housing and Urban Development Act of 1968, loans were limited to owners eligible for occupancy in 221(d)(3)– BMIR projects. The idea was to limit assistance to lower-income families. Many claimed that this was an impediment to renewal efforts, since the owners of improvable property were usually of middle- or upper-income and were ineligible for loans. For this reason, the 1969 legislation changed the income limit to a guideline, and the program may now come to serve the owners of property occupied by low-income families rather than owner-occupants with a low income.

The 115 grant program is closely related to 312; they serve the same areas and are often applied in combination. These are for a maximum of $3,500, though they may not exceed the costs of rehabilitation. If the owner's income is more than $3,000, the grant is limited by the rather complicated provision that it cannot exceed the difference between rehabilitation costs and the maximum loan which could be amortized with housing costs remaining less than one-fourth of monthly income. Thus, 115 grants are restricted to the lowest-income families, and they finance rehabilitation which in all likelihood would not have otherwise occurred.

The performance of the 312 and 115 programs is difficult to assess, since information is scarce. But tentative data are available for the 11,498 owner-occupants who have received loans and the 6,519 who had received grants through January 1969.

Slightly more than half of both the 115 grants and the 312 loans went to urban renewal projects, and the remainder were in code enforcement areas or those areas scheduled for renewal. There have been no loans or grants to families in blighted neighborhoods outside these areas, despite the provision for such activity in the 1968 Housing and Urban Development Act. Administrators claim that there are no plans to extend activity outside of code enforcement and urban renewal areas or to broaden the programs into comprehensive rehabilitation tools.

Under 115, grants averaged $1,871, while 312 loans averaged $5,350; grants can be expected to increase in size since their limit was increased from $3,000 to $3,500 in 1969. The income of recipients and the value of rehabilitated property are given in Table 13.

It is obvious that the grant program is serving the very lowest income families. Loan recipients are better off, with 60 percent having incomes of more than $6,000 annually. Both programs concentrate on properties in the $5,000–$10,000 range, but 44 percent of properties rehabilitated with loans have a higher initial value compared with only 24 percent of those receiving grants.

The small proportion of 312 loan recipients in the lowest-income bracket suggests that grants and loans are not usually combined. This is the case; less than one-fifth of all grant recipients also receive 312 loans. Financial assistance may come from other sources, but the majority of 115 grantees must rehabilitate their property with the less than $2,000 which is typically provided. Obviously, a larger grant is needed to facilitate any extensive repairs. While greater co-ordination with loan programs might increase the number of combined grants and loans, the lower-in-

Table 13. Income of owners and value of property receiving 312 loans and 115 grants, through January 1969

	115 grants	312 loans
Monthly income of recipients		
Less than $250	75%	17%
$250–350	11	9
$350–500	8	14
More than $500	6	60
Value of property before rehabilitation		
Less than $5,000	24%	15%
$5,000–10,000	52	41
$10,000–15,000	16	24
$15,000–20,000	5	10
More than $20,000	3	10

SOURCE: RAA Statistics, Department of Housing and Urban Development.

88

ome families served by grants can probably not afford to go into further debt to rehabilitate, since they are usually mortgaged to the hilt.

The 115 and 312 programs account for more rehabilitations than any other tools, but their assistance is limited geographically and in terms of the repairs which it finances. More costly rehabilitations and those outside renewal and enforcement areas are accomplished under the other subsidy programs. Though rehabilitation is handled in much the same way as new construction, a brief review can help clarify differences in approach.

REHABILITATION UNDER PUBLIC HOUSING

In the public housing program there are two methods of rehabilitation. The most basic approach is for the local authority to purchase existing units and then to finance their improvements, with federal contributions amortizing purchase and rehabilitation costs. These units must be in "adequate" neighborhoods or else where large-scale urban renewal is definitely planned, and the intent is to scatter them in more affluent neighborhoods. Rehabilitation itself is accomplished through the bid and contract method, though in some cases it is done by employees of the authority. Using this direct acquisition approach, 5,798 annual contribution contracts were executed in fiscal 1969, with an average cost of $11,353 per unit, including purchase and rehabilitation. This compared with the $16,246 average for all public housing contracts executed in fiscal 1969; or, in other words, units rehabilitated in this way cost 70 percent of new units, though qualitative differences must be considered.

Rehabilitation can also be accomplished by the turnkey method. As with turnkey-developed new construction, the private firm rehabilitates the project according to certain general standards and sells it upon completion to the local authority. The selling price is determined by the "as is" appraised value of the property plus the estimated cost of rehabilitation, and is thus similar to a cost-plus-fixed-fee (CPFF) contract. Tentative agreements are made by the local authority which guarantee purchase of the completed unit, and this diminishes most of the risk of development. Such a guarantee is needed because rehabilitation costs are much more difficult to estimate than those for new construction, and few private groups would be willing or able to bear the risk of inordinately high costs on any single project. But, under the cost-plus-fixed-fee approach, there is no great incentive for cost or time savings, and the advantages of turnkey are lost. It may be significant that the 838 units accepted for rehabilitation under this method in fiscal 1969 cost $14,137 per unit compared with $11,353 for those rehabilitated under the conventional method. Though turnkey rehabilitations were concentrated in the highest cost areas, the method has clearly been less effective in holding down rehabilitation costs than those for new construction.

THE REHABILITATION OF LEASED HOUSING

The leased housing program is an effective rehabilitation tool. Some 10,600, or 24 percent, of the occupied units leased at the end of fiscal 1969, were rehabilitated. As in the leasing of unrehabilitated properties, the local public housing authority contracts directly with private owners for leases of up to five years. These can be made prior to rehabilitation, and, though its cost must be financed by the owner, the lease guarantee provides an assurance that they will be recovered. This also makes it easier for the owner to obtain outside financing.

Because annual federal contributions are based on the costs of new public housing as opposed to the lower costs of rehabilitated housing, a lease can usually be arranged which will permit the owner to amortize his investment within the lease period. This is an attractive feature to larger-scale tenement landlords, who have access to financing and may be more attuned to the investment guarantees leasing provides than are smaller property owners. Leasing can also be used in conjunction with strict code enforcement, combining sticks with carrots to promote area-wide rehabilitation.

Rent Supplements and Rehabilitation

The rehabilitation component of the rent supplement program has been slow in getting started. By the end of fiscal 1969 only 1,106 rehabilitated units were under payment, although 6,274 were under contract as of September 30, 1969. All but a small number of these contracted units are in the largest cities—Washington, Boston, New York, Cleveland, and St. Louis. Contracted rent supplements were $41 monthly, or less than half of those on new units. The rent supplement works, like leasing, to guarantee a return on rehabilitation outlays. In many details, the rent supplement and leased public housing programs are indistinguishable when applied for this purpose, but there are some differences. Rent supplements concentrate more exclusively on a lower income clientele. In rehabilitated housing, upkeep and maintenance expenses are higher than in newly constructed public housing and, since public housing rents must cover these .costs, leased housing tenants in rehabilitated units must have a slightly higher income than those in new units. Another difference between rehabilitation under the two programs is that the rent supplement program deals exclusively with nonprofit and limited-dividend sponsors, while leases can be contracted directly with profit-making owners. In practice, however, this distinction has been blurred. Though the limited-dividend corporations can realize only 6 percent profit on the 10 percent equity they must put up to secure private loans, some of this equity may be in kind. Landlords may also receive building and maintenance fees and can take accelerated amortization on improvements. In other words, a package can be put together where the profit-motivated landlord will realize up to 20 percent on equity by forming a limited-dividend corporation. But this is cumbersome, and the leased housing program is certainly a more effective tool for dealing with nonresident, profit-motivated landlords. On the other hand, rent supplements should focus on nonprofit or "socially-motivated" limited-dividend corporations undertaking large-scale rehabilitation efforts.

Rehabilitation under 236 and Its Predecessors

The 236 program provides interest subsidies to nonprofit and limited-dividend corporations for the rehabilitation as well as construction of rental units; but, to date, few projects have gotten underway. Of the 3,000 units insured or committed by the end of fiscal 1969, none of which were completed, only 118, or 4 percent, were to be rehabilitated. The performance of the 221(d)(3)–BMIR program is probably indicative of what 236 will accomplish in this area. At the end of fiscal 1969, 6 percent of the 141,992 rental units contracted under the 221(d)(3)–BMIR program were rehabilitated. For the newly constructed units, the average mortgage per unit was $13,941; while for rehabilitated units it was only $12,746. Rehabilitation costs were thus roughly nine-tenths of new construction costs. But this cost comparison must be used cautiously. It makes no allowance for qualitative differences which may exist between the new and rehabilitated units, or for the fact that rehabilitation projects were concentrated in the large, high-cost cities. More than 80 percent of 221(d)(3)–BMIR rehabilitations are in the twenty largest cities, with Boston, Chicago, and New York having 31, 20, and 14 percent, respectively. There are several possible reasons for this geographical concentration. It may very well be that successful rehabilitators require a large-city market where more than one project is available. There are apparently significant savings to be realized through experience and through volume which spreads fixed overhead, and this might explain the fact that 221(d)(3) rehabilitation costs in Boston, Chicago, and New York were lower than the national average, despite their higher new construction costs. In Chicago, for example, with one-fifth of all 221(d)(3)–BMIR rehabilitations, these units had an average mortgage which was 73 percent of that for new construction, compared with the 91 percent figure nationally. Chicago was obviously wise to have a larger proportion of rehabilitated units, and this may be the case for most large cities. Despite these economies of scale in terms of the number of projects, there seem to be no particular savings in individual rehabilitation projects of a larger size. Examination of the 221(d)(3)–BMIR mortgages per unit relative to project size in the largest cities indicated a relatively constant cost. Smaller rehabilitation projects varied much more in unit mortgages, but their average was the same or slightly lower than the average for larger projects. Apparently, the high- and low-cost rehabilitations balance out in larger projects. The 221(d)(3) rehabilitation projects averaged only 68 units compared with 144 in new construction projects. This suggests that many more rehabilitation projects will be needed to supply a given number of units, and the organizational effort will be correspondingly greater than under new construction.

REHABILITATION FOR HOMEOWNERSHIP

The 235 and 235j programs provide interest subsidies on rehabilitated housing sold to low-income families. Rehabilitation under the regular 235 program is handled in the same way as new construction. The owner or nonprofit rehabilitator of a private home simply sells it to a low-income family whose mortgage payments are subsidized. In the case of a private owner, there is no special incentive for rehabilitation since his selling price is the market value of his home, with or without rehabilitation, though without improvements he may not be able to find a buyer. Nonprofit sponsors may rehabilitate single-family units for resale, usually dealing with less than four units at a time. In the fourth quarter of fiscal 1969, roughly 4.5 percent of the existing units insured under the regular 235 program were substantially rehabilitated, which would mean less than 400 since its beginning. Based on this limited experience, substantial rehabilitations of single-family units on a one-shot basis do not appear very profitable or attractive to private interests and require a great deal of organizational effort per unit by nonprofits.

The 235j program is a much more useful instrument for rehabilitation of single-family units, since it deals with larger nonprofit groups and emphasizes multiple-unit rehabilitation. The nonprofit organization or public body receives an FHA-insured market rate mortgage covering the acquisition and rehabilitation costs of an entire project, which must consist of at least four units needing improvement, though they do not have to be substandard. Once rehabilitated, the units are sold, with the project sponsor providing individual mortgages to finance the purchase. These mortgages bear a market interest rate, but the purchaser is required to pay only 20 percent of his monthly income, with the remainder contributed by the government.

As yet, only a handful of 235j projects are in development, and the experience of the 221h program which it replaces is helpful in estimating its future impact. The former program provided direct BMIR loans rather than interest subsidies, but in most details it was comparable. Through September 1969, 4,187 units had been committed for rehabilitation under 221h. Not unexpectedly, more than three-fourths were in metropolitan areas with over 100,000 population. Few were located in more affluent neighborhoods, with four-fifths in blighted areas or core cities. This should be avoided under 235j; the rehabilitation of single units in blighted areas is not a wise strategy unless it is part of an over-all effort to save or restore the neighborhood, since the surrounding blight makes the preservation of isolated "good" homes difficult. Under 221h, the typical family was large, having 5.7 members. As with new housing built for homeownership, experience has shown that one- and two-bedroom rehabilitated units are much less popular than three- and four-bedroom units. Since young and elderly couples usually prefer rental housing, homeownership rehabilitation should focus on larger units for larger families.

APPLYING THE REHABILITATION TOOLS

These, then, are the major rehabilitation tools. There are five programs essentially for the rehabilitation of single-family housing. The 312 loan and 115 grant programs serve individual low- and moderate-income homeowners in code enforcement and urban renewal areas. The 235j and 221h are mostly used for small groups of around 10 to 20 units rehabilitated by nonprofit organizations for resale, while regular 235 can provide for the rehabilitation of individual units.

The rehabilitation of rental housing is promoted on a larger project basis by the 236 program, aimed at the "professional" nonprofit and limited-dividend groups which have a continuing interest in housing, since the interest subsidy is best used on larger projects. Public housing acquisition and rehabilitation is needed for these larger projects when experienced private groups do not exist or when closer integration with renewal efforts is desired. Turnkey development will work where a rehabilitation industry is well established, but it is generally not a very good tool. Rent supplements are most useful in combination with 236 or other rehabilitation efforts. Alone, they have been used on projects of a medium size of around 20 to 40 units, which are manageable by the less-experienced nonprofits. Leased housing is a good way of reaching private landlords and prompting them to rehabilitate. It is probably a more useful tool for this purpose than rent supplements packaged to offer attractive returns on investment.

The particular mix of programs depends on local conditions, such as the quality and location of the housing stock, the availability of private financing, the strength of the code enforcement and urban renewal efforts, and the quality of the local public housing authority and of private housing groups. Much more than in new construction, the character and cost of rehabilitation varies from area to area and from project to project. Minor roofing repairs or replacement of the plumbing and heating facilities may be sufficient to make a unit habitable. In other cases, the interiors must be completely gutted and replaced and costly structural repairs made. Rehabilitation can involve limited work on a single-family unit in a rural area or the massive renovation of whole blocks of central city multi-family units. In the first case, assistance may be needed directly by the low-income homeowner, while in the second it must be provided for large-scale purchases by a third party or directly to nonresident landlords. If rehabilitation is to succeed on a large scale, programs are needed for all these purposes, and their uses must be carefully co-ordinated so that problems will be met in a rational rather than in a makeshift way.

9
Rural Housing

The subsidy programs discussed so far are administered by HUD and are used almost exclusively in urban areas. Rural conditions differ in significant ways, and these differences undermine the performance of HUD's tools, requiring specially adapted programs.

A major obstacle is the low level of development of rural financial markets. In many rural communities the local bank is the only financial institution, and its resources are usually limited. Insurance companies and savings and loan associations, which provide most of the housing credit in urban areas, are much less in evidence. An unpublished study by the Department of Agriculture estimated that banks account for 30 percent of all mortgages in rural counties compared with less than 14 percent in SMSA's; life insurance companies and savings and loan institutions account for 36 percent as opposed to 72 percent in urban areas.[1] Because banks are limited by liquidity requirements and

[1] Department of Agriculture, Economic Research Service, "The Housing Situation in Rural Areas." Mimeographed, p. 8.

federal and state banking laws as to the amount of assets which may be held in mortgages and because the large mortgage institutions are not active there is a rural credit shortage. Interest rates are high and terms usually unfavorable. As a result, programs relying on private sector financing, such as 235 and 236, are likely to have much less success in rural than in urban areas. Financing must often be provided directly by the government if it is to be available for low-income housing.

A second characteristic of rural areas is the preponderance of single-family, scattered-site units. In 1969, 96 percent of all rural families lived in detached homes, compared with 68 percent of families in SMSA's, and the population density was only 15 per square mile as compared with more than 3,000 in urban areas. Dispersed populations mean that large-scale, single-family developments and multi-family rental projects will be impractical in most cases. Rental assistance programs can thus have only a limited impact and programs which rely on economies of large-scale financing or construction are not likely to be successful.

A final impediment to housing programs in rural areas is the severity of the need itself. With 30 percent of the nation's population, they have almost half of its poor. Since poverty thresholds are lower, these poor have less cash income than those in urban areas, and if adequate housing is to be provided, more of the cost may have to be borne by the government. Demographically, these poor are also the most difficult to house. A large proportion are elderly and would normally occupy rental housing, which is not feasible. Many others are in large families, who are always more difficult to house. And a large number are among the more than 400,000 migrant farm workers who must occupy a number of units during the course of a year.

Special tools are needed to overcome these obstacles, and Congress has fashioned several assistance programs especially for rural use. These have been delegated to the Farmers Home Administration of the Department of Agriculture, and though they fall far short of rural needs, they have had a much larger impact than HUD's programs.

THE 502 RURAL HOUSING PROGRAM

The major rural housing instrument is the 502 program, providing loans for the purchase, improvement, and construction of homes. The majority are used to purchase new homes and thus to increase the rural housing supply, but a substantial proportion are also for purchasing or improving existing units. In fiscal 1968 two-fifths went to buy existing homes requiring an average of only $400 in repairs. Another 3 percent were for refinancing and repairs averaging $1,150 per unit; 6 percent were for repairs alone, amounting to an average of $3,700. One highly praised but limited use is for self-help. In fiscal 1969, 693 insured 502 loans, averaging $8,245, were used to purchase materials which individuals or self-help groups used themselves.

Most 502 loans are insured, with only 2 percent coming from a direct loan fund, but this loan insurance is far different from that under HUD's programs. Because of the shortage of local housing credit, the Farmers Home Administration provides the loans initially and continues in their administration, selling an offsetting amount of "participations" to the private sector. The participations are government-guaranteed, and have no connection as far as the purchaser is concerned with any mortgages which were made. Thus, 502 "insured" loans are for all intents and purposes direct loans, with their own source of funding.

The 502 loans have an interest rate which is determined on the basis of need, but there are no exact standards. Measurable salaries and wages make up much smaller portions of income than in urban areas, and need must be individually determined. The applicable interest rate is decided at the local level by one of the 1,700 FHA county committees. Roughly 10 percent of loaned funds carry a market rate and go to those in the "above-moderate" income category; these do not provide any very significant subsidy. Low- to moderate-income families—mostly those with incomes of less than $7,000—receive the bulk of loans which have an interest rate of 5 ⅛ percent. Additional interest credits are available for poorer families, and approximately one-ninth of all 502 recipients are presently given subsidies below the 5 ⅛ percent rate. In fiscal 1969 this amounted to 5,535 families receiving these additional interest credits.

The income distribution of borrowers receiving BMIR loans is given in Table 14. The striking aspect of this breakdown is the small proportion of what would normally be called "low-income" families receiving loans and interest subsidies under the 502 program. The poverty threshold for a farm family of six is $4,000, but only 13.5 percent of all BMIR loans went to families with less than this income. If the cost of living in farm areas is 15 percent less than that in urban areas, as the poverty threshold assumes, 50 percent of recipients earn more than $6,000 annually, or what would be comparable to at least a $7,000 income in urban areas. Clearly, rural housing assistance under 502 has focused on a relatively more affluent group than the urban subsidy programs.

THE 504 REHABILITATION LOAN FOR THE RURAL POOR

For those with extremely low income and with questionable repayment ability, the Farmers Home Administration uses the 504 rather than the 502 program. This provides direct loans at a 1 per-

Table 14. Family income of recipients of 502–BMIR loans

Number of borrowers	42,616
Average family income	$5,793
Percent distribution of borrowers by family income	
Under $3,000	5.3%
$3,000–3,999	8.2
$4,000–4,999	14.4
$5,000–5,999	22.7
$6,000–6,999	26.6
$7,000–7,999	16.3
$8,000–8,999	4.2
$9,000–9,999	1.3
$10,000 and over	1.1

SOURCE: Farmers Home Administration, Department of Agriculture.

cent interest rate with up to ten years to repay; these loans are made to owner-occupants for essential repairs. The maximum amount of assistance is only $1,500, which rules out any major improvements, but the loans can pay for plumbing, roof repair or the minor structural improvements which may be needed to make a dwelling livable. In fiscal 1969, 5,048 of these loans were obligated, mostly going to the poorest of the poor and averaging $1,105 each. It is unlikely that the homes were substantially improved with such a small amount of rehabilitation, but it is equally unlikely that poor owner-occupants could have repaid the loans needed for major repairs.

Rental and Co-operative Housing under 515 and 521

Most 502 and 504 loans go to the least populated rural areas. More than half of both are for farms or households in open country, while less than 14 percent of 502 and 10 percent of 504 loans going to places of 2,500 to 5,500 population. These small rural communities are served more directly by the 515 and 521 programs providing loans for the development of rental and co-operative housing, respectively. The loans are insured by the Farmers Home Administration as under the 502 program, though some are made directly. Individual developers can participate, receiving 5 ⅛ percent loans; and nonprofit organizations and co-operatives can benefit from additional interest credits, reducing their rate to as low as 1 percent, depending on the size and income of occupant families. Due to the shortage of experienced organizations, individual developers received three-fifths of the loan funds committed in fiscal 1969. Housing co-operatives have played only a small role, with two loans in fiscal 1969 accounting for only 1 percent of obligated funds. Altogether, there were $17.3 million in initial and subsequent obligations in fiscal 1969, subsidizing roughly 2,000 units. The proportion occupied by lower-income families is not known, but since the units which were individually developed do not receive large subsidies, they are unlikely to serve the poor. This means that, at most, 1,000 rental or co-operatively

101

owned units were provided for lower-income families through the 515 and 521 programs in fiscal 1969.

FARM LABOR HOUSING

There are two programs which concentrate specifically on the housing needs of domestic farm workers, the 514 loan program and the 516 grant program. The loans can be made directly to farm-owners or farmers' associations, to private nonprofit organizations, and to state or local governments. They bear an interest rate of 5 percent, and have a repayment period of up to thirty-three years. The grants are limited to government bodies or broadly based nonprofit groups, and are provided from direct appropriations. As of December 31, 1968, $13.7 million in loans and $9.3 million in grants had been approved, and these had been used to provide 3,903 family units and 3,175 dormitory slots. In fiscal 1969, loan obligations amounted to $3.5 million, and grants to $5.0 million, so that probably less than 1,500 family units and 1,000 dormitory slots were provided in fiscal 1969.

RURAL ASSISTANCE UNDER 235

Finally, administration of the 235 homeownership program in rural areas is delegated to the Farmers Home Administration. There are minor differences in property standards and credit underwriting, but basically it is the same as the regular 235 program, with the government contributing interest subsidies on loans made by private mortgagors directly to low-income borrowers. So far, this program has had little impact. Tight money has intensified the normal credit stringency in rural areas, and most 235 loans have been made through GNMA and FNMA tandem purchases. As of November 17, 1969, only 134 new and 273 existing units had been financed in rural areas under 235, although the volume is picking up somewhat.

But 235 may be more important in the future if Operation Breakthrough can lead to mass production economies. Since most rural construction is on scattered, open sites, land costs are minimal. Construction and material costs account for most of the price of housing, and few economies of scale are presently realized in purchasing, planning, or building in rural areas. The conditions would appear to be ideal for factory-built housing. In testimony before Congress, board chairman James R. Price of the National Homes Corporation—the largest builder of prefabricated homes— claimed that his corporation can presently supply new homes, including land and furnishings, for $12,500 in Southern cities.[2] Loans for comparable dwellings have averaged $12,000 under the 502 program, and this does not include land costs and furnishings. Transportation is surprisingly cheap for prefabricated units, and it is not at all optimistic to presume that the larger-scale production will result in further economies. Rural areas may benefit from these savings through the 235 program, especially if the government continues to provide a market for its mortgages through the GNMA and FNMA.

The Failure to Assist Low-Income Families

One of the obvious problems with the Department of Agriculture's subsidy programs is that only a small proportion goes to lower-income families. It was estimated that in fiscal 1969, 5,000 to 6,000 units were constructed or substantially rehabilitated for low-income families receiving interest credit under the 502 program; 5,000 were improved with 504 loans; maybe 1,000 were provided under the rental housing program; no more than 3,000 minimal living spaces were built under the labor housing grant and loan programs; and approximately 100 new units of 235 housing were financed. The total of roughly 15,000 units is dwarfed by the number constructed or substantially rehabilitated for similar low-income families under the urban assistance programs in fiscal 1969.

[2] James R. Price, Statement Before U.S. Congress, House, Subcommittee on Housing of the Committee on Banking and Currency, *National Housing Goals*, 91st Cong., 1st Sess. (Washington: Government Printing Office, 1969), p. 444.

The traditional whipping boy is the Farmers Home Administration, and certainly some of the criticism is deserved. But, given the severe credit shortages in rural areas, it is understandable that the Farmers Home Administration would ration its limited funds among the many in need of assistance. Its responsibility is not limited or directed to the poor, and even if it had given more emphasis to their needs, let us say doubling the proportion of 502 program funds going to lower-income families, the assistance gap between rural and urban areas would be little changed for those with the greatest needs.

However, if rural housing assistance programs are to be expanded, and if they are to focus on the needs of the lowest-income families, the FHA system may indeed become an obstacle. There are 1,700 local committees of the Farmers Home Administration which execute its loan programs. While these committees may be extremely effective in weighing the personal characteristics of loan applicants, they are rarely experienced in the housing field and are far less capable of organizing and co-ordinating local housing efforts. Organization and co-ordination are essential, since rural areas lack the variety of profit, nonprofit, and quasi-government housing groups which can be found in urban areas, and if emphasis is shifted to the provision of housing on the basis of need alone, as it must be, the system is not very good. This does not mean that rural housing programs must be transferred out of the Department of Agriculture and into HUD, although this is a possibility which should certainly be given consideration; it only means that a specialized staff will have to be developed, familiar with rural conditions and yet also familiar with all aspects of the housing market. Funds will have to be increased and earmarked for assistance to low-income families in rural areas.

10

The Impact of Housing Assistance

There are three aggregate measures of housing assistance activity: (1) the number of additional units provided for low-income families each year; (2) the total stock of units which are being subsidized; and (3) the level of subsidy on these units. Roughly speaking, these are measures of the growth, scope, and depth of housing assistance.

The needs of the remaining ill-housed are met by increasing the number of subsidized housing units. New construction adds directly to the stock of adequate low-cost housing. Rehabilitation may also increase this stock, if substandard units are salvaged, but often it merely upgrades the quality. The lease and purchase of existing units do not add to the physical quantity of housing, but they increase its availability to the low-income families. Together, new unit construction, rehabilitation, and existing unit acquisition determine the number of additional families who will be helped.

Since the Housing and Urban Development Act of 1968, federal policy has focused on "production," which includes "substantial" rehabilitations and new construction. Subsidized production starts have expanded markedly in the last three years, reaching their highest total, as illustrated in Chart 2. This production is broken

105

CHART 2

SUBSIDIZED HOUSING PRODUCTION

Units in Thousands

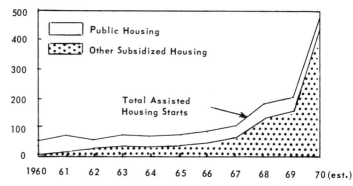

Source: Department of Housing and Urban Development.

down by program for 1968 and 1969 in the following table, with their shares of total production giving some indication of their relative emphasis in the housing strategy.

Between 1968 and 1969 there were important changes in emphasis, and these are especially important since 1968 and 1969 are the first years of large-scale escalation of the assistance effort and suggest the evolving patterns of emphasis in the housing strategy. For instance, while public housing starts increased by 4 percent between the two years, those developed with conventional methods decreased by one-fourth, indicating the shift to turnkey. The 235 and 236 programs increased their share of HUD's production from almost nothing in 1968 to 11 percent in 1969. The 221(d)(3)–BMIR program was drastically curtailed, with a 30 percent reduction, as it was phased out in favor of 236; but the 202

Table 15. Production of assisted housing units

	1968				1969			
	Total	Percent of all	Starts	Rehabilitations	Total	Percent of all	Starts	Rehabilitations
Public housing	59,700	31	56,700	3,000	65,700	29	59,100	6,600
Conventional	(42,300)	(22)	(40,800)	(1,500)	(36,100)	(16)	(30,200)	(5,900)
Turnkey	(17,400)	(9)	(15,900)	(1,500)	(29,600)	(13)	(28,900)	(700)
Leased housing	7,200	4	2,500	4,700	16,000	7	6,400	9,600
Rent supplements	16,900	9	16,500	400	17,800	8	17,100	700
236 Rental	—				10,400	5	10,100	300
202 Elderly	6,600	3	6,400	200	7,400	3	7,400	—
221(d)(3)–BMIR	51,000	26	45,400	5,600	35,900	16	32,400	3,500
235 Homeownership	100	—	100	—	8,700	11	8,300	400
221 h	700	—		700	1,700	1		1,700
115 & 312	9,700	5	—	9,700	11,800	5	—	11,800
Total HUD programs	151,900	78	127,600	24,300	175,400	78	140,800	34,600
U.S.D.A. programs	43,200	22	34,000	9,200	48,200	22	38,600	9,600
Total assisted production	195,100	100	161,600	33,500	223,600	100	179,400	44,200

SOURCE: Department of Housing and Urban Development.

housing program for the elderly increased slightly despite the anticipation that it, also, would be replaced by 236. The Department of Agriculture's rural programs increased production by 14 percent, but their proportion of all assisted housing decreased slightly to approximately one-fifth.

Along with these new and rehabilitated units produced annually, additional low-income families are assisted each year in the units acquired directly from the housing stock through public housing acquisitions, through leasing, or through 235 assistance. Nearly one-fifth of all units made available for occupancy in fiscal 1969 were existing without rehabilitation, and these are not included in production figures.

The number of additional units assisted each year is determined by the annual budgetary authority of the various programs. For all but the direct loan programs, contract authority is provided which limits the annual payments made on newly assisted units and thus restricts the number of contracts for such payments. As an example, annual contributions on the public housing contracted in any year cannot exceed the authority for that year. In the case of direct loans from a revolving loan fund, money can become available through the repayment of past loans or through direct appropriations; together these create new loan authority. Thus, some 202 loans can continue out of repayments even if there are no additional appropriations.

Contract authority for the major assistance programs administered by HUD is assigned to four separate categories: (1) low-rent public housing, which lumps together leased housing authority as well as conventional, turnkey, and acquisition public housing authority; (2) the rent supplement program; (3) the 235 home-ownership program; and (4) the 236 rental housing assistance program which includes some converted 202 and 221(d)(3) commitments. The 312 and 115 program levels are determined separately, the first, with is own loan fund and the second, through an administrative allocation. Table 16 was prepared by HUD for the four large subsidy categories, based on the Nixon budget for 1971. If this proposal is accepted, HUD's contract authority will increase,

Table 16. HUD's major assisted housing programs, amounts becoming available for contract authority

(In millions)

	1969	1970	1971
Public housing	$147	$225	$170
Rent supplement program	30	50	75
Homeownership assistance program	70	90	140
Rental housing assistance	10	85	145
Total contract authority	$357	$450	$530

SOURCE: Department of Housing and Urban Development.

but to a much smaller degree than in fiscal 1970. There will be a marked shift away from the public housing program toward the private-sector oriented 235 and 236 programs, whose authority is expanded by even more than in the preceding fiscal year. Additionally, there will be a loan authority of $45 million under 312 in fiscal 1970, and $35 million in fiscal 1971.

The effects of these contract authorizations on reservations and starts were estimated by HUD for each program in Table 17. There is obviously a lag between changes in reservations and those in starts. For instance, 221(d)(3)–BMIR reservations will be reduced by three-fourths between fiscal 1970 and 1971, while starts will decrease by only 60 percent; similarly, the increase in 236 starts will lag behind contract authority increases. But the changing priorities implicit in the contract authorities are quite clearly reflected in the reservations and starts under the different assistance programs.

The rural programs will also increase their activity. Direct and insured loan commitments for low- and moderate-income housing will increase from $469 million in fiscal 1969 to an estimated $829 million in fiscal 1970 and $1,484 million in fiscal 1971. This rapid expansion of authority is expected to result in the increasing unit commitments shown in Table 18.

Table 17. Unit reservations and starts by fiscal year under HUD's programs

	Unit reservations			Unit starts		
	1969	1970	1971	1969	1970	1971
Low-rent public housing, including leasing						
New or rehabilitated	82,310	99,000	99,500	79,246	102,000	100,000
Existing without rehabilitation	(27,571)	(9,000)	(6,500)	(—)	(—)	(—)
TOTAL	(109,881)	(108,000)	(106,000)	(79,246)	(102,000)	(100,000)
Rent supplement[a]	16,523	15,300	30,300	16,632	22,000	14,000
Below market interest rate	30,877	18,500	4,500	44,668	30,000	12,000
Housing for the elderly (202)	5,313	4,300	1,900	6,965	7,000	5,800
Rental housing assistance (236)	21,637	133,100	141,700	997	16,500	77,000
Homeownership assistance (235)						
New or rehabilitated	23,005	123,000	133,600	2,715	48,000	144,600
Existing without rehabilitation	(4,698)	(21,900)	(14,900)	(—)	(—)	(—)
TOTAL	(27,703)	(144,900)	(148,500)	(2,715)	(48,000)	(144,600)
Rehabilitation loans and grants	10,947	16,885	23,900	10,663	16,292	23,199
Inventory increase	190,612	410,885	435,400	161,886	241,792	376,599

a Unit reservations reflect only the market rate portion of the rent supplement program. Total unit reservations for the rent supplement program are:

1969	18,905
1970	46,700
1971	68,100

SOURCE: Department of Housing and Urban Development.

Table 18. Low- and moderate-income housing programs administered by the Farmers Home Administration

		(estimated units counted in thousands)	
Program	*1969* *(actual)*	*1970* *(est.)*	*1971* *(est.)*
New construction	24	48	100
Rehabilitation	10	15	20
Rural rental housing	2	2	4
Farm labor housing	1	1	2
235 new or rehabilitated housing	1	2	7
Subtotal	37*	69*	133
Purchase of existing housing	10	15	20
Total, rural housing for low- and moderate-income families	47*	84*	153

SOURCE: The Budget of the United States Government, Fiscal Year 1971.
* Totals not exact because of rounding.

THE STOCK OF ASSISTED HOUSING

These annual increases in the subsidized housing stock are only the tip of the iceberg. The total number of units receiving assistance at the end of fiscal 1969 was more than five times the number which had been added during the year. It is the assisted housing *stock* which determines the number of households being helped, while the annual starts determine how many more will be helped in the future. Table 19 presents rough estimates of the cumulative total of subsidized units available for occupancy at the end of fiscal 1969.

These data indicate the overwhelming importance of public housing. Even if emphasis is shifted to private sector production, public housing will continue to be far and away the most vital program in terms of the numbers it serves. This suggests the importance of improving its operations and maintaining its subsidies. The other striking figure is the large percentage of assisted units under the 221(d)(3)–BMIR program. Despite its apparent unpopularity, and even though it is being phased into 236, 221(d)

111

Table 19.   Assisted housing stock

	Estimated number of units available for occupancy at end of fiscal 1969	Percent of total
Public housing	740,600	64%
Leased housing	44,000	4
Rent supplement only	23,000	2
221(d)(3)–BMIR	91,000	8
202 elderly	26,200	2
Homeownership	5,500	—
Rehabilitation loans and grants	20,600	2
Rural programs*	202,700	18
Total	1,153,600	100%

* This is an estimate of the units provided for occupancy under the loans outstanding at the end of fiscal 1969.
SOURCE: Individual program data.

(3)–BMIR has made a substantial contribution to the assistance effort. Considering the large number of tenants now residing in housing assisted under this program, it is unfortunate that less data are made available on its operations. The rural programs also account for a large share of assisted units, but very little subsidy is provided and only a small proportion are occupied by families living in poverty.

Because production has increased rapidly since the 1968 Housing and Urban Development Act, the stock of assisted units can be expected to grow rapidly in the next few years, with changes in composition reflecting earlier changes in emphasis. Table 20 gives the best estimates which can be made of completions through fiscal 1971. The projected distribution of occupied units at the end of fiscal 1971, compared with that at the end of fiscal 1969, indicates the smaller but still highly significant role of public and leased housing programs, the rapid growth of 235, and the continuance of the rural share at around one-fifth of all assisted units. The data are extremely crude, and more specific conclusions should not be drawn.

Table 20. Unit completions and existing acquisitions *(In thousands)*

	Fiscal 1969	*Fiscal 1970*	*Fiscal 1971*	*Cumulative for occupancy in fiscal 1971*	*Percent of total*
Public housing, including lease	82.6	93.0	100.0	977.6	55%
Rent supplement	11.2	18.0	22.0	53.0	3
221(d)(3)–BMIR	34.0	40.0	25.0	156.0	9
202	5.9	8.0	8.2	42.4	2
236	—	16.0	19.1	35.1	2
235	5.5	21.3	120.5	165.5	10
Rehabilitation loans and grants	10.1	15.7	22.5	58.8	3
Rural	34.4	47.1	109.1	283.3	16
Total	183.7	259.1	426.4	1,771.7	100%

SOURCE: Department of Housing and Urban Development.

THE LEVEL OF HOUSING SUBSIDIES

These stock and flow figures combine housing units subsidized under the 504 rural program through the negligible BMIR savings on its $1,100 average loans with those receiving more than $1,000 annually in direct subsidy payments under public housing. Quite obviously, these are not comparable. The average subsidy under each program must be considered in weighing their contributions to the housing effort and in estimating the aggregate federal housing subsidy.

Under the major ongoing programs of HUD, the average and total subsidy is not difficult to compute, because the payments must be directly appropriated. Table 21 presents the payments appropriations, with fiscal 1971 data coming from the Nixon budget proposal.

The average subsidy is the total appropriation divided by the number of assisted units. On an annual rather than fiscal basis, HUD has made the following estimates of average subsidies (see Table 22). They vary markedly from year to year, depending on

113

Table 21. Payments appropriations for major HUD assistance programs

(In millions of dollars)

	1969	1970	1971
Low-rent public housing, including leasing	$379.6	$480.0*	$654.6
Rent supplement program	12.0	23.0	46.6
Homeownership assistance program	3.8	23.5	84.0
Rental housing assistance program	3.2	3.0	20.6
Total payments appropriations	$398.6	$529.5	$805.7**

* Includes proposed supplemental of $13.6 for 1969 and $6.5 million for fiscal 1970.
** Total not exact because of rounding.
SOURCE: Department of Housing and Urban Development.

interest rates, construction costs, tenant incomes, and other exogenous variables, and for public housing, they do not include the indirect subsidies from tax-exemption of local bonds.

The subsidies under the other housing assistance programs are much more difficult to estimate. In the 202, 221(d)(3)–BMIR, 312 and rural programs, the loans are more or less direct and there is no annual appropriation which can be translated straightforwardly into a subsidy amount. The BMIR subsidy on these loans depends on the interest rate which would otherwise exist, and this is variable and difficult to estimate. It could be argued that the true subsidy is the difference between the BMIR and the federal borrowing rate, but the FHA rate is a better proxy for the rate the

Table 22. Average subsidy for units under payment in year

	1968 actual	1969 estimate	1970 estimate
Public housing programs			
Conventional (including older units)	$406	$438	$481
Conventional (new)	708	745	769
Turnkey	822	687	767
Acquisition and rehabilitation	645	631	654
Leased housing	779	805	820
Rent supplement	636	816	900
Homeownership	—	756	756
236 rental	—	744	744

SOURCE: Department of Housing and Urban Development.

borrower could otherwise get. Use of the FHA rather than federal borrowing rate will yield a higher computed subsidy. Quite obviously, estimates of average and total subsidies can only be made in the roughest ways.

Under 202 and 221(d)(3)–BMIR, the subsidies are probably less than those of 236, since their BMIR is higher and since their tenants probably have a higher average income than those of 236. The average subsidy in 1969 was probably in the range of $500 to $700 per unit under these programs, as compared with the estimated $744 under 236. Multiplying these figures by the 125,000 202 and 221(d)(3)–BMIR units at the end of fiscal 1969, the total subsidy is in the neighborhood of $62.5 to $87.5 million, though probably closer to the lower figure.

Under the 312 program, there were approximately 10,000 loans outstanding at the end of fiscal 1969, with an average value of $5,350. Much of the principal may have been retired, but at most the annual subsidy did not exceed the $2.5 million BMIR savings on the total amount. There were approximately 3,000 grants in fiscal 1969 under the 115 program, for a total of some $5.5 million in subsidies.

The rural programs are large in terms of the number of assisted units, but their subsidies are small relative to HUD's programs. The average 502 loan to low- and moderate-income families was a little over $10,000 in fiscal 1969. With an interest reduction from 8 ½ percent to the 5 ¼ percent BMIR, this would imply an annual subsidy of only $325 per unit. Roughly one-eighth of all loans are subsidized to a lower interest rate, but the average subsidy is probably only slightly more than $325. The other major rural program is 504. With its average loan of $1,105, and its 1 percent BMIR, 504 gives a subsidy of less than $100 annually per unit. Total housing subsidies under the two programs can be estimated from the quantity of rural loans. At the end of fiscal 1969 there were $1.3 billion outstanding loans to low- and moderate-income individuals. If an average BMIR of 5 percent can be assumed, and a market rate of 8 ½ percent, these would account for a total subsidy of $45 to $50 million. The farm labor and rental loan programs accounted for only $26 million in outstanding loans between them, which would mean less than a million dollars in subsidies.

All of these estimates are, of course, extremely crude, and this type of analysis deserves more careful attention elsewhere, but it yields at least a ballpark estimate of the total federal housing subsidy. In fiscal 1969 it amounted to approximately half a billion dollars. This will necessarily increase as the housing programs are expanded, and their average subsidy is increased. For instance, in HUD's four major programs alone—public housing, rent supplements, 235 and 236—payments appropriations are projected to be $805.7 million in fiscal 1971. In the early seventies, the total housing subsidies will reach more than $1 billion.

11

Issues Related to Housing Subsidies

Behind these facts and figures on program performance lie a number of highly controversial issues concerning subsidy techniques and program priorities. Five of the currently most important are: (1) the effectiveness of rehabilitation and the emphasis it should be given relative to new construction; (2) the need for and relative cost of homeownership subsidies as opposed to the more traditional rental housing subsidies; (3) the feasibility of dispersing low-income units outside the central city and the desirability of helping the ill-housed in rural areas; (4) the use of the subsidy programs to bring about cost-saving changes in construction techniques; and (5) the provision of subsidies for occupancy in existing rather than newly-constructed units.

The Role of Rehabilitation

There is continuing debate over the problems and potential of rehabilitation, and over its role in the housing effort relative to new construction. On the one hand, it is clearly cheaper than new construction. Under the assistance programs which have both components, average rehabilitation costs have been significantly less, even though most are concentrated in the high cost urban areas.

117

For instance, through fiscal 1969, 221(d)(3)–BMIR rehabilitations cost 91 percent of newly constructed units, while rehabilitations under the acquisition program during fiscal 1969 averaged only 70 percent of the normal public housing cost. HUD has also sponsored careful studies of projects in New York City, one of the few market areas with enough units to permit some degree of generalization; these covered 6,184 units of new construction in 21 projects, and 890 rehabilitated units in six projects. The cost of newly constructed units, with deductions for all but the barest essentials, averaged $20,120 or 44 percent higher than the rehabilitated unit cost, even though these stripped down units would probably have been inferior to those which were rehabilitated. Construction times on the rehabilitation projects were much shorter.[1] Available data generally support the favorable appraisal of Victor De Grazia, of Chicago's Kate Maremount Foundation.

It seems to be too little realized that rehabilitation of structurally sound buildings anywhere in the country can be cheaper, quicker, and easier than demolition and new construction even before the human costs are totaled up. From the experience of the Kate Maremount Foundation, new construction under the 221(d)(3) program costs in Chicago about $15,000 per unit, as against $10,000 for rehabilitation; new construction in New York costs about $17,000 and rehabilitation $12,000. The new construction figures assume written-down land; the rehab figures assume private purchase.

Speed is also important. Give me three million dollars to rehabilitate 300 units and give someone else whatever he needs to relocate residents and to demolish and build 300 new units; if we both have the same breaks, I will beat him to occupancy not by months or weeks, but by years. This will be true in practically any city in the country.[2]

Despite the relative success of completed rehabilitation projects, a comparatively small number have been undertaken. Rehabilita-

[1] Department of Housing and Urban Development, "Cost and Time Associated with Tenant Rehabilitation in Manhattan, New York City" and "Cost and Time Associated with New Multifamily Housing Construction in New York City" (Washington, D.C.: Government Printing Office, 1968 and 1969).

[2] Urban America, Inc., *The Ill-Housed* (Washington, D.C.: Urban America Inc., 1969), pp. 23–24.

tion is much more difficult to implement than clearance and new construction, since private groups which can successfully rehabilitate do not exist in most areas. Incentives can be created for new construction and the market will react to them. The government can provide interest subsidies to private lenders, can promise market rents on a given number of units in a project, or can offer to purchase new units on a turnkey basis, with the reasonable expectation that lenders, nonprofit organizations, and builders will react. But the rehabilitation industry—if it can be called that—is extremely fragmented. Most large builders and lenders have thus far shied away. Nonprofit groups are inexperienced and cannot call on experienced contractors. Resident owners of slum property are usually unaware of federal subsidy programs and are not reactive to market incentives. And nonresident landlords are making a very good profit letting their property deteriorate, making it hard to convince them to do the opposite.

Active efforts to overcome these obstacles can be productive. In a few large cities, particularly New York, Chicago, Cleveland, Los Angeles, Detroit, Boston, Washington, Philadelphia, and Pittsburgh, the federal and local governments have worked to make rehabilitation succeed. Nonprofit groups and professional rehabilitators in these cities have improved their methods and reduced their costs substantially. For instance, the Alleghany Housing and Rehabilitation Corporation (AHRCO) of Pittsburgh, one of the nations most experienced rehabilitators, reduced average unit costs from $11,000 on its first project, to $9,800 on its second, $8,900 on its third, and $8,600 on its fourth. Other groups may not duplicate this success, but experience is clearly important.

The federal government must play a more active, catalytic role if additional cities are to participate in rehabilitation on a large scale. Substantial and continuing resources must be guaranteed specifically for rehabilitation, and the government must work to organize and support groups who can effectively use them. If this happens, city halls will have more reason to increase code enforcement and alter tax laws, and large construction companies will be much more likely to undertake rehabilitation, joining nonprofit and

119

limited-dividend groups. To make this commitment and to provide the needed organizational impetus, the rehabilitation components of the separate programs should be brought together and funded as a unit. The variety of tools is needed, but they must be administered under a separate appropriation so that there will be an incentive to rehabilitate rather than just to build new units. With such change, rehabilitation can be highly effective.

Despite this potential effectiveness, rehabilitation is currently being de-emphasized. The first policy statement on housing goals issued under the Housing and Urban Development Act of 1968 prescribed that two of the six million subsidized units to be produced over the decade were to be rehabilitated. This goal was reduced in the second annual policy statement, being cut in half to one million units. The justification was that rehabilitation costs had risen, that few cities were found to have large blocks of units for which rehabilitation would be economical, and that entrepreneurial capacity was limited and would take time to expand. These justifications are questionable. Rehabilitation costs have certainly risen, but so have the costs of new construction. Given the apparently wide difference between the two as late as fiscal 1969, it is very unlikely that rehabilitation has become uneconomical. The claim that few cities have large blocks of rehabilitatable units is contrary to the evidence of thousands of abandonments of structurally sound dwellings in the larger cities. It is also rather misleading since the experience under the rehabilitation projects so far has been that there are few economies of scale in rehabilitation, and that single buildings can be restored as efficiently as whole blocks. The crucial factor is the shortage of entrepreneurs and the nature of the beast is such that if money is made available for rehabilitation, the supply will expand in short order.

The reason why rehabilitation has not been more successful is that the effort has not been adequately funded or administered. The meager results to date are certainly no proof that rehabilitation will not work, or that it cannot presently provide the third of subsidized housing units originally envisioned. With its proved cost advantages, and its potential for even further improvements,

120

rehabilitation seems a wise investment. We must learn to conserve as well as construct if we are to meet our housing needs.

THE ROLE OF HOMEOWNERSHIP

Until 1968 only a handful of low-income families had received subsidies to purchase homes. The rural and rehabilitation programs had helped a substantial number of those already owning their homes, but they assisted few to become homeowners. The 235 program was really the first homeownership subsidy effort. With its rapid success and wide popularity, homeownership was suddenly accepted as a major goal of housing assistance. Its priority has dramatically increased, so that the revised housing goals call for 2.95 million units to be produced for homeownership between 1970 and 1978, compared with 2.85 million rental units. To expedite this increased production, the Administration has proposed to expand the scope of 235 and to permit local public housing authorities to build units specifically for sale.

The popularity of 235 made it obvious that low-income families can want and can benefit from homeownership—that their desires are little different from the 60 percent of American families who own their homes. A careful survey of 103 low- and moderate-income families in Detroit found that 59 percent wanted to own a single-family home, including 42 percent of those with an income below $7,000.[3] They wanted homeownership for the same reasons as most of us—privacy, space, the security of continued occupancy, and, most important, the equity which could be accumulated. Homeownership can be a substitute for a savings program, and this is especially important to low-income families.

Perhaps the greatest evidence of demand for homeownership among low- and moderate-income families is the rapidly expanding mobile home market. In 1969 the impressive total of 389,000 new mobile homes were sold. For many, this is the only feasible

[3] Frank and Mary Sengstock, "Homeownership: A Goal For All Americans," *Journal of Urban Law*, vol. 46, issue 3, University of Detroit.

type of ownership. A HUD survey in 1968 found that slightly over 70 percent of the families in new mobile home units earned less than $8,000, and 45.6 percent earned less than $6,000.[4] Most of these are in the eligibility range for the 235 program, and though some may prefer mobile homeownership, many would have purchased conventionally built homes if they had been available at a lower price. In 1970 an estimated 500,000 mobile units will be put in place, which indicates a substantial demand for low-cost, owner-occupied housing and for government assistance to low- and moderate-income homebuyers.

A large number of families are apparently willing to pay more for the benefits of homeownership. The average family income of 235 recipients was roughly $4,500 after deductions, and, as the calculations for Boston showed, such families would pay approximately one-third of their income for debt retirement and maintenance expenses. Rental housing is available, at least in theory, for one-fourth of income under other assistance programs, and yet many families are willing to pay the difference.

Despite this evidence that low-income families have a strong desire for homeownership and are willing to make sacrifices to own their homes, federal policy did not respond until recently because of, among other things, the belief that homeownership subsidies would be too costly. Such assistance would necessarily concentrate on single rather than multi-family units, and it was assumed that these single-family homes would be more expensive because of higher land and construction costs per units.

It is not at all clear, however, that new rental units can be provided more easily or cheaply than single-family housing. In terms of land use, townhouse construction on small sites sometimes costs less than the necessarily larger-scale acquisition of property for apartment buildings. As for construction costs, they are far different when expressed in terms of cost-per-person-housed than in terms of cost-per-unit. According to a HUD survey, families mov-

---

[4] Department of Housing and Urban Development, *Housing Surveys* (Washington, D.C.: Government Printing Office, 1969), p. 91.

ing into new, owner-occupied units in 1968 average 4.2 members, compared with a 2.5 average for new rental units. Though owner-occupied units cost 20 percent more, they housed nearly 70 percent more people.[5]

Evidence from the comparable 235 and 236 assistance programs raises similar questions about the savings in building rental units. The average mortgage on the 4,000 Section 236 units committed or insured as of June 30, 1969 was $16,100 compared with a typical mortgage of $15,350 on newly constructed 235 homes; the latter housed five members per unit, while the former will probably house closer to three on the average. The estimated subsidies in fiscal 1970 will be $756 per unit under 235, compared with $744 under 235, so that the costs are not much greater in assisting equity accumulation by low-income homebuyers.

Cost and demand factors are not the only considerations suggesting a greater emphasis on homeownership assistance; there are also a host of social benefits which might result. Homeowners are considered more stable than renters, and if low-income families become homeowners, they may also become more stable. One pecuniary effect is that homeowners are more likely to invest in their property. In 1967 expenditures for maintenance, repairs, and improvements on owner-occupied units were roughly one-third higher than on those which were renter-occupied. The argument that homeowners make more money and can afford these expenditures has some weight, but considering the overwhelming evidence that even in blighted areas owner-occupied dwellings are better maintained on the average than those with nonresident landlords, it seems safe to assert that more widespread ownership will help slow down the deterioration of the low-cost housing stock.

Increased emphasis on homeownership would also mean increased attention to the needs of larger families, and this is sorely needed. In 1966 there were approximately 900,000 poor families with five or more children, and these families contained almost half of the children living in poverty. And yet even in public hous-

---

[5] *Ibid.*, pp. 12 and 83.

ing, which is the only program to serve them to any appreciable extent, only 16 percent of tenant households had five or more children in 1967, and only one-third had five or more members. In the other rental assistance programs, the picture is even worse where maximum cost limits do not allow adequate adjustments for family size, and concentration on performance in terms of "units built" has shifted emphasis away from the number of people housed in these units. The median family size in 235 units to date has been five members, and, if for no other reason, homeownership assistance should be expanded to meet the needs of similar large families among the ill-housed.

The Location of Subsidized Units

The geographical distribution of assisted units to a large extent determines who is helped and how effectively. The decision of where to build is a vital one. But it is also very complex. The economic prospects of potential locations must be weighed, as well as the distribution and mobility of those in need. The availability and price of land are important, and the unfortunate reality of income and racial discrimination cannot be ignored. All these factors must be considered in distributing units and subsidy funds, and to do this, regional and local conditions must be known. No hard and fast rules can be laid down. However, two general issues must be faced at the national level: first, the emphasis which will be given to helping rural areas with their distinct and serious problems; and, second, the effort which will be made to penetrate more affluent neighborhoods, especially the suburbs.

The first issue is relatively clearcut. By almost any measure, rural areas receive a disproportionately small share of housing assistance. In 1960 they contained 60 percent of all substandard housing, and 36 percent of all overcrowded units, yet they received only a meager portion of all housing assistance. At the end of fiscal 1969 they had less than one-tenth of all public housing units and an almost insignificant share of the units built under the other assistance programs administered by HUD. The Department of Agriculture's rural assistance programs do not make up for this imbalance, since they serve mostly middle- and upper-income clientele with their limited funds.

Rural housing needs have been slighted for many reasons. Substandard rural housing is hidden from view and easily ignored, and many believe that open spaces make up for inadequate shelter. Another reason is the misconception that housing problems will solve themselves through migration. This is not likely since rural migration rates are slowing and since those left behind are the least able to afford adequate shelter. The relatively immobile low-income families remaining in rural areas need help where they are.

The federal government has to play a much more active and direct role in rural areas, since they generally lack the private institutions which will react to the refined incentives of the urban programs. Direct funding on a larger scale, and increased organizational effort are needed.

This increased emphasis is warranted, not only by the severity of needs and the inequity of the present distribution of assistance, but also because it may be cheaper to house families in rural areas. Land costs less and is more readily available, and there is a great potential for mass-produced, single-family homes. If substandard housing is to be eliminated within the decade, a vastly increased supply of subsidized units will be needed in rural areas.

The really tough locational decision is the amount of effort which should go to dispersing low-income, central city populations. Since almost all urban public housing had been and still is located in the central city, the new private sector programs were launched with the intent of penetrating suburban neighborhoods and those within the city which are more stable. Low-income occupants could then benefit from contact with more affluent families and the use of their community facilities. Unfortunately, success has been limited. Only 12 percent of the subsidized rental units in process under 221(d)(3), 236, and the rent supplement program as of January 15, 1970, were in the suburbs. The 235 program has given indications that it will do better, but clearly the disper-

125

sion of low-income and Negro populations to date has not lived up to expectations.

⟡ Opposition to low-income housing continues to be strong in more stable neighborhoods. There are three very intractable motives for exclusion: (1) additional low-income families with children increase the local tax burden; (2) there is a basic preference for income homogeneity and a desire to demonstrate success through segregation from the less affluent; and (3) racial discrimination is still prevalent, along with fears that low-income and Negro residents will depress property values. The policies which would mitigate these motives lie outside the housing assistance programs. Racial discrimination can be countered to some extent by stricter enforcement of fair housing laws, but until public attitudes are changed, integrated housing will not be pervasive. The fear of higher taxes or property value losses can be overcome by grant-in-aid bonuses or through the shifting of responsibility for public services to a higher level of government, but these changes take time and are not likely to be made in the near future. And the desire for socio-economic homogeneity will be difficult if not impossible to overcome; in all the housing programs it has been the experience that racial mix is easier to achieve than income mix. All this adds up to the fact that subsidy programs stressing or providing inducements for suburban locations are not likely to succeed on a large scale. This is a fact of life, and as unattractive as it may be, it must be accepted until changes are made in public attitudes and in other facets of public policy. The 1970 legislative proposals of the Nixon Administration would remove the requirement for local government approval of subsidized housing locations, and though this change is needed, its passage is as unlikely as the prospect of its being used to force suburban locations on a large scale if it were passed. Central city locations will continue to predominate for assisted housing because of exclusion in the surburbs, and the subsidy programs should not be placed in the vanguard of the effort to break down housing discrimination, since they would undoubtedly be the first casualty.

126

The cost and availability of land in the central city is thus a matter of critical importance. Fortunately, there is evidence that land shortages will not be a problem in most central cities, at least in the next decade. The Douglas Commission found large tracts of unused lands which could serve as locations for low-income housing. In central cities whose SMSA's had a population of over 250,000 in 1960, 12.5 percent of their land was undeveloped; and for those in SMSA's of over 100,000, it was 22.3 percent.[6] There are also large areas which could be converted from other uses, including government-owned lands, those cleared under urban renewal, riot-torn and decayed districts, and underutilized tracts such as railroad sidings and junkyards. If nothing else, the presently substandard and overcrowded housing occupied by low-income families could be rehabilitated, or replaced with high-rise units, and little additional land would be needed. Though there are serious drawbacks to high-rise living and concentrations of the poor, more amenities could be designed into multi-family projects. Thus, central city lands are available to meet the subsidized housing needs of at least the next five or ten years, though these may not be as cheap or preferable as suburban locations.

Where central city locations are feasible, as they will be in most cases, a very touchy issue is whether the attempt to penetrate suburban areas should be permitted to delay the construction of subsidized units. This can easily happen; for instance, some public housing projects have been held up several years because of controversies over site location. Certainly the subsidy programs should try to break down income and racial discrimination, but, on the other hand, this effort should not take precedence over action to build adequate housing, even if it must be in the central city.

[6] The National Commission on Urban Problems, *Three Land Research Studies, Research Report No. 12* (Washington, D.C.: Government Printing Office, 1968), p. 20.

REDUCING COSTS

Until recently the subsidy programs had done little to improve the organization of the housing industry or its production techniques. Operation Breakthrough was a first step in this direction, using 236 funds for experimentation with new building techniques. But much more could be done. With some 250,000 starts and rehabilitations annually, the subsidy programs have a potentially great market power which could be applied to bring about needed changes. To do this, the obstacles to cheaper housing must be identified and strategies designed to overcome them.

The Douglas and Kaiser commissions concluded that housing costs could be significantly reduced without drastic changes in industrial organization or building techniques. Cheaper methods of production are known and tested, but have not been adopted throughout the industry; costs are consequently higher than they need be. There are three major obstacles to their implementation: outmoded building codes, union opposition, and unrealistic or purposely restrictive zoning laws. Where restrictive work rules and building codes combine to limit the use of prefabricated materials, costs are raised measurably. Freedom to use prefabricated components and wall panels would result in a saving estimated to be between 2 and 5 percent of total cost. Zoning laws often restrict large-scale low-cost housing projects, especially in suburban areas where they are more feasible. As the postwar Levittowns showed, there are substantial economies associated with larger-scale suburban developments, and these also exist for multi-building rental projects, where multi-building costs can be between 5 and 15 percent less per unit according to experience in New York City.[7]

More widespread use of prefabrication and larger-scale projects could result in cost reductions of as much as 10 percent, given the present organization of the industry and presently available construction techniques. Potential savings of this order of magni-

[7] Department of Housing and Urban Development, "Cost and Time Associated with New Multifamily Housing Construction in New York City" (Washington, D.C.: Government Printing Office, 1968), p. 43.

tude cannot be ignored, but even greater savings are likely from a more drastic reorganization of the housing industry. Through the use of factory-produced sectionalized units, the cost of the average single-family home could be reduced substantially, more than 15 percent according to one estimate for Toledo, Ohio.[8] And these are only a part of the possible savings from industrialized production. It is already feasible to factory-build and transport completed homes, and indications are that these are even cheaper than sectionalized units. The largest builder of completely prefabricated housing, the National Homes Corporation, claims that completed units cost 10 percent less than those built from prefabricated sections, because of the economies of mechanized factory production. The plant of the National Homes Corporation in Lafayette, Indiana, has a capacity of 9,000 units annually, which are intended mainly for Chicago markets. New York and several other cities could provide a market for similar plants, and regionally located facilities could serve cities in a radius of almost 300 miles as judged by current experience.

The only type of industrialized housing which is presently manufactured on a large scale is the mobile home. These clearly demonstrate the savings in factory production and the willingness of lower-income families to accept totally prefabricated construction. The rather startling fact is that mobile home output amounted to over 28 percent of new, conventionally built, single-family homes produced in 1967, and are probably close to half in the current housing slump. The reason is obvious. Three-fourths of mobile homes sold for less than $7,000, and 94 percent for less than $10,000 in 1967, compared with 6 percent of all new one-family homes selling for less than $12,500 in 1966.[9] There are obvious differences between mobile and conventional homes in size, quality, and durability, but mobile home accommodations have improved greatly. Surveys indicate that almost half of mobile homeowners

[8] The National Commission on Urban Problems, *Building the American City* (Washington, D.C.: Government Printing Office, 1968), p. 436.
[9] Department of Housing and Urban Development, *Housing Surveys* (Washington, D.C.: Government Printing Office, 1969), p. 69.

actually prefer their style of life to conventional homeownership, and the rapidly expanding sales demonstrate that in the consumer's judgment, even with their disadvantages, mobile homes are the best buy around.

Nevertheless, mobile homes are not a panacea for low-income housing needs. Their potential in the central city and in more densely populated suburban areas is limited. As presently designed, they are impractical for large families. And though they are better constructed and more livable than they are often credited, permanent and more spacious single-family homes are undoubtedly preferable.

There are many obstacles to producing industrialized housing with characteristics similar to those of conventional units. All those mentioned relative to the use of partial prefabrication techniques apply doubly to factory production. Local building codes will have to be modified before industrialized housing can be introduced into many areas, and agreements must be worked out with the building trades unions, since factory labor will be substituted. Some public education will be needed for wide acceptance, although this factor is probably overrated, since the alternative for low-income families is usually substandard or over-crowded housing. Without these changes at the local level, industrialized housing cannot succeed. But these alone do not assure its success. There are still two overwhelming obstacles to its mass production: the fragmentation of demand and cyclical instability.

If a single plant has a capacity of 9,000 units annually, there must be a market for these units within economical shipment distances of the plant—currently estimated as 300 miles at the most. Many such market areas exist, if the plant can count on maintaining a substantial share of the low-cost housing built within this radius. National Homes built its Lafayette plant only after the assurance of the Mayor of Chicago that the city would purchase 5,000 units annually. But such guarantees are difficult to get elsewhere. No one can guarantee a market for unassisted low-cost units; and the administration of the subsidy programs is usually divided among many local governments, agencies within

130

these areas, and a variety of sponsoring groups, so that subsidized purchases are also difficult to co-ordinate.

A related obstacle is the wide fluctuation in demand, especially at the regional and local level. Large-scale production, which would require massive capital expenditures, cannot be undertaken unless demand is guaranteed for an extended period, but localities presently have no way of knowing what they will need and be able to finance more than a year ahead.

To realize the economies of mass production, comprehensive measures must be taken to insure a large and predictable market. The leverage of all the housing subsidy programs must be used to aggregate demands and to stabilize their fluctuations at regional and local levels. This will require longer-range commitments and greater co-ordination of the programs by city halls and state governments. If these goals were pursued vigorously, local problems could be easily overcome. Federal building standards could be used on all subsidized projects, and few if any cities would refuse assistance as a matter of principle. Labor agreements could be worked out, using the very real leverage of stable and certain demand. Such leverage should be exerted because of the substantial cost reductions which can result.

The Use of Existing Housing

The housing subsidy programs concentrate on the production of new units to meet the needs of the ill-housed. Assistance has been linked to the development process, and in only a small number of cases are subsidies given for occupancy in existing and unrehabilitated housing. Under the 235 homeownership program, 9,000 of the first 16,000 assisted units were from the existing housing stock, but the proportion is decreasing and the FHA has declared that no funds will be available for such assistance in 1970. Only 5 percent of the public housing units accepted in fiscal 1969, or a little over 3,000, were purchased without rehabilitation. And the leased housing program, which more than any other em-

131

phasizes the use of existing standard housing for low-income families, provided only 69 percent of its first 44,000 units through direct lease without rehabilitation; this proportion is declining, with half of the units targeted for fiscal 1970 to be supplied through new construction. Besides this small and declining proportion of assisted units under these three programs, there are only a handful of other subsidized dwellings which were acquired directly from the housing stock.

The reason for this de-emphasis is the fear of inflation. Subsidies for existing units do not increase the stock of housing directly; they merely increase the demand for available standard units, raising their price. Lower-income families will be better housed, but others will be squeezed out by higher prices, and housing markets will become tighter. In times of inflation and housing shortages, such effects are particularly undesirable, and because of rising prices and falling vacancy rates HUD has drastically reduced subsidies for existing units.

Questions can and should be raised about this policy, despite its appearance of utmost economic rationality. Subsidies for existing units have many comparative advantages: the families are housed more quickly since there are no construction lags; costs are almost always less than new construction, so that subsidies need not be as high; and it is easier to penetrate more affluent neighborhoods by acquiring existing units than by building new, low-income housing. All of these positive features must be balanced against the possible inflationary effects, and to reject this approach only because it will cause inflation is to count the costs without the benefits.

The extent and duration of the inflation which would result from existing unit subsidies under the present programs should not be overestimated. For instance, if emphasis were continued at its past level in the 235 program, this would mean that approximately half of the 48,500 unit starts scheduled for fiscal 1970 instead be existing units, which would mean the purchase of .03 percent of the estimated housing stock. It would take many years for such small additions to demand to have a noticeable inflationary effect, even if there were no vacancies and no new construction. This may not be too much of a price to pay, since a large number of low-income families could be housed more cheaply and quickly, and hopefully in better neighborhoods. The issue is certainly not as clearcut as the dramatic de-emphasis of existing unit subsidies would seem to indicate.

There are, in fact, many arguments for a general housing allowance, available to all families on the basis of need, and applicable to existing as well as newly constructed units. This could not be implemented until inflation eases and housing construction picks up, but it would have many advantages.

A housing allowance would attack the problem through the housing stock as well as through annual additions to this stock. The total quantity of adequate housing is more than 40 times the usual yearly production, and this could be redistributed to eliminate most of the problems of the ill-housed. A more equitable distribution of housing is certainly as justified as the goal of more equitable distribution of income.

The housing allowance would also be more comprehensive than the present strategy. The Kaiser Commission estimated that there were 7.4 million families in this country in 1967 whose incomes were so low that they could not afford adequate shelter. Roughly speaking, this is the universe of need for housing allowances. Not all of these families live in substandard dwellings, and not all would require standard units if they were given a subsidy, since, in 1960, only 36 percent of the units occupied by poor families were substandard. For the two-thirds of low-income families who live in standard housing, the housing allowance would free income for other necessities.

Prices will rise if the housing allowance is instituted, though it is impossible to estimate the amount or duration. The physically ill-housed who are subsidized will be able to bid for and occupy adequate units, and this will raise housing costs for all unsubsidized families. But the unsubsidized families are also the ones who must pay, at least indirectly, for housing subsidies. The costs of inflation are worth the reduction in subsidy levels, since low-income families will move into older and cheaper units, and subsidy costs per family will be less than if new units were provided. It is the more affluent families who will be pressured into buying new units, and this is much more rational than supplying them for low-income occupancy. Experience and empirical evidence point to the fact that richer families have a greater preference for new housing, while those with low-income are more concerned with its basic qualities other than age or stylistic features. The families who must pay for housing subsidies are probably better off giving housing allowance for occupancy in cheaper and older units and moving themselves into more expensive, new units.

Even though these long-run benefits may justify the housing allowance approach, the majority of households will be faced with higher prices and housing shortages; this is a difficult pill to swallow when the patient is already suffering from an overdose. Public acceptance will only come when the concern over inflation has eased and housing production has picked up, when society is finally committed to eliminating the housing problem, and when there is visible proof that the theoretical advantages of the housing allowance will bear out in practice. As the Kaiser Commission recommended, a large-scale experiment is needed to test and demonstrate the efficacy of housing allowances.

But, even without such experiments, it is clear that the assistance programs providing subsidies on existing units—the 235 homeownership, public housing acquisitions, and leased housing programs—could and should be expanded, with more emphasis given to the purchase of existing homes under 235 and the rental of existing units under leased housing.

12

Program Improvements and Priorities

Federal housing assistance has expanded and grown more complex. For the first twenty-five years of such efforts, public housing was the only subsidy tool. Though it was gradually modified to serve low-income families more effectively, other approaches were needed which would provide alternative subsidy techniques, would utilize the resources of the private sector, and would reach the ill-housed not served by public housing. In the sixties, a number of new subsidy programs were initiated, providing a potentially comprehensive tool-kit to meet low-income housing needs. These tools have been applied with mixed emphasis and success, and experience has led to improvements in their design and application. Further refinements will be possible as more data become available and experimentation proceeds, but the programs as a whole have demonstrated their effectiveness. More subsidized units are being produced than ever before, and this production entails a variety of approaches and meets a variety of needs.

Because there are alternative techniques and goals, priorities must be determined. The present funding of the different tools represents one set of priorities. Others are possible, and indeed seem warranted by careful analysis of the housing programs and problems.

135

Whatever priorities are chosen, an assortment of approaches and techniques must continue to be used. Low-income housing needs are complex and require a variety of tools for their most effective solution. Attempts to consolidate the existing programs and to simplify the assistance effort must be carefully considered to insure that needed options are not foreclosed. Though some tools must be improved, others discarded, and still others added, the kit of tools which has been developed over the thirty-five years of housing subsidies must continue to be well-stocked and comprehensive.

USING AND IMPROVING AVAILABLE TOOLS

The public housing program has been drastically revised, and further changes are clearly needed; but it must continue to be the mainstay of the assistance effort. Despite an increasing emphasis on other programs, it still accounts for by far the largest share of starts, and an overwhelming majority of all occupied units. There has been a shift within the program to turnkey development, justified by its favorable cost and time characteristics. Turnkey development increases private sector participation, but the government still has more control over the type of housing which is built and the way in which it is operated than it does under any other subsidy program. For this reason, public housing has been able to serve the families who are most in need of help and least attractive to private sponsors, developers, and property owners under the other programs. There are inherent problems in serving such a clientele. For instance, local authorities had found that rising maintenance and operating costs could not be met from the rent their tenants could pay. Though these difficulties will probably be eliminated by the 1969 amendments providing additional federal contributions, many other problems remain, especially those dealing with the qualitative aspects of public housing construction and operation. As in other welfare programs, increasing confrontation appears inevitable between newly organized tenant and welfare groups and the rather stodgy local authorities. The present administrative organization of public housing needs careful re-consideration. In the largest cities, permanent and professional authorities might be established, with closer ties to the city government and more responsive to organized community groups. Elsewhere, HUD may have to take a more active role through incentive programs or through more explicit control, dealing directly with tenant groups and improving the conditions to which they object. However, it must be recognized that any program trying to serve the lower-income clientele of public housing will face the same serious problems. There is no reason to believe that private builders and developers will be more effective than local authorities in designing and operating housing for this group. The reason for public ownership in the first place is that the private sector cannot provide for the lowest-income families and has been insensitive to their needs. Yet the current de-emphasis of public housing is an attempt to shift such problems back to the private sector. Public housing can be improved, and an improved program is better than any private sector effort which could be designed to serve the lowest-income families.

The leased housing program can also be an effective tool; but despite its popularity and substantial achievements in terms of subsidized units its role should be clearly circumscribed. Leasing should not be used for new housing where turnkey or conventional public housing development are feasible .The latter are a better investment of federal dollars, enabling public rather than private equity accumulation and permitting greater flexibility and control over housing policies. However, in the case of "as is" or rehabilitated dwellings, leasing can be effective, providing adequate housing more cheaply and directly than new construction. The inflationary pressures caused by leasing, with assisted families competing for and raising the price of a limited supply of housing, are not likely to be great, since the number of leased units in any particular market area will be small. If leasing must be curtailed in some places because of tight housing conditions, it should be available for much greater use when private starts begin to rise and the current situation eases. But, in all likelihood, leasing could presently be expanded for existing and rehabilitated units with no ill effects, and this is an effective way to subsidize the housing costs of low-income families.

The rent supplement program was initially intended as a complement to the leasing program; it was anticipated that rental guarantees would stimulate the construction of new low-cost units, while leasing would improve the utilization of units already in existence. But increased emphasis on new construction under the leasing program has obliterated the distinction between the two. Where new construction is involved, the rent supplement program is probably a better tool than leasing. Because of its longer-term guarantees, and the fact that its sponsors are socially motivated, rent-supplemented units will more surely go to low-income families over their life. Rent supplements are restricted to nonprofit or limited-dividend sponsors, and low-cost housing can apparently be built without the profit incentives of the leasing program. Though rent supplement projects are more difficult to initiate, they will work if the program is adequately funded. However, before the rent supplement program becomes generally effective its cost limits will have to be revised. Greater emphasis should also be put on the use of rent supplements in conjunction with the interest subsidy and BMIR programs, to help them reach a lower-income clientele. This double subsidy has proved to be one of the most effective ways of mixing incomes in assisted projects.

The other major rental assistance program is 236, initiated to replace the 221(d)(3)–BMIR and the 202 programs for the elderly. It is an effective substitute for 221(d)(3)–BMIR, since it will be able to reach a lower-income clientele, will utilize private resources to a greater extent, and will lead to more business-like practices among sponsors. It is not as good a substitute for the housing program for the elderly; to date, unit costs have been higher and there has been criticism that its approach is less adapted to the needs of the elderly and to the abilities of interested nonprofit groups. The arguments seem to have validity, and 202 should be continued as its reauthorization in the Housing and Urban

Development Act of 1969 permits. The use of 236 funds to experiment with cost-saving techniques under Operation Breakthrough is certainly warranted, but more comprehensive efforts are needed. There is little being done outside of Operation Breakthrough to use the market power of the federal subsidy programs to foster needed changes in the homebuilding industry; in fact, the assistance programs have lagged in adopting new, cost-saving techniques. Two measures are clearly needed: first, a stable and predictable level of assistance rather than the highly arbitrary pattern of the past; and second, regional and local aggregation of assistance demands to support the mass production of low-cost housing and to force unions and local governments to make needed improvements in their building practices. Operation Breakthrough was launched to achieve these specific objectives, but its "sticks and carrots" are too small to produce the desired changes. The effort aims at testing industrialized housing designs rather than testing industrialized production; and it is in the latter area that greater potential economies exist rather than in the development of new materials or techniques.

Homeownership is facilitated for the "rich poor" and moderate-income families under the 235 program, and there is little doubt that this option should be available. Nevertheless, the 235 program is not the most effective tool which could be designed to provide assistance for homeownership. With the added payments needed to meet maintenance and operating expenses, the family in 235 housing must often pay a greater portion of its income than if it were assisted under 236. This higher cost might be justified if the equity build-up under 235 were substantial, but this is not the case. Under the interest subsidy technique, the terms of the mortgage are based on the market interest rate, and equity accumulation is much slower than it would be under a direct loan at a reduced rate. The 235 program is also misdirected in its attempt to finance the acquisition of new units only, with limitations on the proportion of existing units which can be assisted. Existing units are easier and cheaper to acquire

139

and more immediately available. The purchase of "as is" or rehabilitated housing should certainly not be discouraged, and should probably be encouraged.

Rehabilitation is a component of all of the assistance programs, but usually a very minor one. The separate and solely rehabilitation programs are limited, and total rehabilitations are nowhere near the one-third proportion of all assisted units anticipated in the 1968 housing legislation. Before the rehabilitation effort can be expanded, the programmatic tools must be improved and coordinated and their application rationalized. Turnkey rehabilitation, for instance, should not be stressed since the guarantee needed by the developer undermines its value and since capable private developers exist in only a few areas. Leasing and conventional public housing are more valuable tools; the first assures the rehabilitator that his property will be rented and outlays will be returned without financing the costs themselves, while the second provides the needed centralized control and permits large-scale efforts in conjunction with urban renewal and slum clearance. The 312 and 115 programs, which are the major tools strictly for rehabilitation, provide too little assistance for the major repairs needed to salvage many deteriorating or marginally substandard units. Loans to low-income homeowners may not be effective because repairs have little relationship to their income or their ability to repay. A combination of grants and loans may be needed, but only a small portion of 312 and 115 loans and grants are being used together.

Assistance to rural areas is extremely limited under HUD's programs, and those of the Department of Agriculture hardly compensate for this imbalance. HUD's tools often do not work because conditions differ in rural areas. Financial institutions are limited and private mortgage funds scarce; large-scale builders do not exist which could take advantage of incentive programs; populations are scattered, ruling out rental assistance for the most part; but most significantly, poverty is proportionately worse in rural areas where low-income families have so little income that they fall below the minimums under most HUD programs.

Separate tools are needed which recognize these problems and are able to overcome them, but the Department of Agriculture's rural assistance programs are not presently the answer. Its large number of loans under the 502 program must be discounted by the fact that the BMIR is only a little less than the market rate and the subsidy much smaller than under 235 or 236. Only a small proportion receive special interest credits which make the subsidy comparable with that under HUD's programs. The 1 percent BMIR of 504 loans provides a deeper subsidy, but the loans are so small that substantial improvements cannot be made. The Farmers Home Administration has used its lending authority to serve middle- and upper-income rural families rather than those who are poor or near poor. Its reasoning has been that the individuals receiving loans must have an adequate income to repay them—an argument which would prevail under any loan program where loans are made to individuals. Some alternative subsidy technique is needed in rural areas.

Suggested Priorities

Priorities must be decided in some way so that housing funds can be divided among the competing programs, approaches, and clienteles. The underlying choices are difficult—much more difficult than making the claim that all the programs could use more money, which they could. But funds are limited, and choices must be made. Four priorities are listed below based on the analysis of the last chapter.

1) The highest priority should be given to meeting the needs of rural areas. With by far the most severe low-income housing problems, these areas receive a disproportionately small share of federal funds. The Department of Agriculture's programs give most of their assistance to middle- and upper-income families, while HUD's subsidies barely reach outside of urban areas.

The millions of ill-housed in rural areas must be helped. It is naive to expect migration or the urbanization of rural areas to solve these problems, and special efforts will be needed. Though

141

HUD's programs can and will be applied with greater success, it will be a long time before they make a dent in rural needs. The Department of Agriculture's tools must be made to serve lower-income families, and they must be drastically expanded.

2) Greater priority is being given to homeownership, and this seems warranted. There is a very definite imbalance in the present stock of assisted units, with almost four-fifths being rental housing, and this should be corrected. Lower-income families can benefit as much from ownership as families of higher income. Single-family homes are better adapted to the needs of larger families, and homeownership assistance may be one of the best ways to help the "deserving poor" who work full-time but live in poverty because their families are so large. On a per-person basis, this approach may be cheaper than rental assistance, and it is almost a necessity in the rural areas with the greatest need. Home-ownership assistance should be expanded as the new housing goals intend, with subsidies being provided for the purchase of existing as well as new units as housing production picks up generally.

3) Rehabilitation is being de-emphasized, and this is a mistake. From the available evidence, it seems fairly clear that where re-habilitation can be organized on a multi-project basis by a single sponsor, significant economies can be realized which make it markedly cheaper and faster than new construction. The necessary organization and co-ordination has not been provided at either the national or local level, except in a few cities which have partici-pated heavily. Other large cities could duplicate their success if funds were provided and the rehabilitation programs co-ordinated. In other words, rehabilitation can succeed with organization, and the original goal that one-third of all subsidized units be rehabilitated is worth pursuing.

4) Under those programs with authority to subsidize low-in-come occupancy of existing units, this authority has been quietly de-emphasized. The claim is that since vacancy rates are low, such measures would have an intolerable inflationary effect. But the in-flationary effect has never been demonstrated because no city

has had a large subsidy program relative to its housing stock. Given the higher vacancy rates in many areas of the cities, and given the fact that most cities presently have few units of existing housing which have been subsidized, this approach could be greatly expanded even under present conditions. It should be, because the results are immediate and much cheaper than building new units. As inflation eases, and housing production picks up, a much more general housing allowance might be tried. A housing allowance would permit lower-income families to compete for existing standard units, reallocating the housing supply, and pushing more affluent families into the purchase of new units. Hopefully, this would lead to newer units being built for families of higher income, while low-income families would receive subsidies to occupy cheaper, existing units.

Redirecting Housing Policy

The program improvements and priorities which were outlined suggest the directions in which we should be moving. Unfortunately, many of these run against the current of recent developments.

One of the primary goals of the present Administration is the simplification and consolidation of the subsidy programs. This was apparent in the administrative reorganization within HUD, and it is even more obvious in the Administration's 1970 Housing and Urban Development Act proposal. This bill would divide the subsidy programs into four basic groups: (1) the subsidized homeownership program, which would be the same as 235, though 20 percent of funds would be reserved for larger subsidies to especially low-income families; (2) the subsidized rental program, which would parallel 236, with 20 percent of funds allocated for the very poor in place of rent supplements, which would be terminated; (3) the public housing rental program, which would be little different from the present program except that rentals in every case would be based on the income of tenants; and (4) the public housing homeownership program, which would extend Turnkey-III sales of public housing to tenants, and would permit local authorities to develop new public housing for sale to low-income families.

While this consolidation appears reasonable, and is made even more attractive by association with needed cost limit and subsidy level changes, it has serious weaknesses. Necessarily, new rules and guidelines would have to be created, just when sponsors and private participants are adjusting to those of the newer programs. There is a high cost in confusion and delay related to substantial program changes or reorganizations, and it is not clear that there are enough advantages in the new proposals to justify this cost.

The proposed legislation would terminate both the 202 and rent supplement programs. As indicated, 202 seemed to be doing a better job for the elderly than 236. The rent supplement program has been successful, given its fiscal constraints, and it has important advantages over leasing in providing guarantees for the construction of new units. In dropping the rent supplement program, and extending the income range of the other tools, the bill would move away from the situation in which separate programs were directed to separate income groups, fitting together to cover the range of need and allowing emphasis to be placed on any desired group through the funding of its program. The rent supplement program served the lowest-income families, and though other programs would be extended downward to serve this group, experience has shown that programs end up serving those nearest their maximum limits. There is no guarantee that after the rent supplement program is eliminated the lowest-income families will receive as great a proportion of assistance.

The whole thrust of the consolidation effort may also be misdirected. Renaming and limiting the number of programs does not alter the need for a variety of incentives and subsidies to deal with different clienteles, sponsors, types of housing, and geographical areas. Reform will simplify organizational charts and legislative expositions, but it will not change the complexity of the low-income housing problem or the need for options and refinements within

144

the subsidy programs. All it will do is to internalize the complexities, side-stepping the problem of defining the specific uses of the present programs and assigning priorities to their specific goals. This would give administrators much more responsibility for techniques and priorities, reducing congressional oversight and control. The possible consequence is that administration will become less rather than more informed, since most of the information about the housing programs is generated to satisfy congressional needs. For instance, appropriations for the leasing program are contained within the over-all public housing appropriation; a separate, detailed justification is not required or offered. As a result, neither Congressmen nor administrators have a very exact idea of who the program is serving, or what its comparable cost features are. In contrast, there is a wealth of information about the similar rent supplement program which has its own appropriation, and its administration is much more conscious. Separately funded and separately administered tools are needed if the complex housing problems are to be effectively met.

There are other current developments which are opposite to the recommended directions of change. Public housing is being de-emphasized, with private programs being expanded to meet low-income needs and with the sale of public housing units being advocated to side-step management problems. Many of public housing's problems are being solved, but rather than attempting to solve those which remain we are turning to other approaches of unproved and questionable ability to serve the low-income public housing clientele. Public ownership and control are currently considered a burden rather than the very definite asset which they can be.

Rehabilitation is also being de-emphasized for little apparent reason. Given current housing shortages and limited funds, the cost and time advantages of rehabilitation should have their greatest weight, and the shorter life associated with rehabilitated units is of less importance, since they can be replaced by newly produced units when conditions are more propitious. But, rather

145

than expanding and funding the organizational effort needed to make rehabilitation work, the government has emphasized the less difficult but more costly route of new construction.

The subsidization of existing units has also been discounted, out of fear of the inflationary effects. The whole housing effort continues to be inverted, subsidizing new and costly construction for the poor rather than placing them in adequate existing units. The large stock of housing could be used more effectively to meet low-income needs, and this approach could be expanded with few inflationary effects.

Finally, rural needs continue to be ignored. The USDA programs are expanding and improvements in HUD's operations will provide further assistance, but there is still an outrageous imbalance in the geographical distribution of housing assistance funds. More resources are needed specifically for rural areas and specifically for their lower-income families, and these needs should receive the highest priority.